Recovering from Adverse Childhood Experiences and Becoming the Best Version of You!

First Edition

Giulia Preziuso, LMHC

It's Your Mother's Fault—Now What?

Printed by B.C. Allen Publishing and Tonic Books
144 N 7th St. #525
Brooklyn, NY 11249

Now taking manuscript submissions and book ideas at any stage of the process:

submissions@tonicbooks.online

Printed in the United States of America

Editor:
Cover Design: Maria Alcoke
Interior Design: Susan Veach

ISBN: 978-1-7366361-0-7 (Paperback)
ISBN: 978-1-7366361-7-6 (ePub)

"Giulia is just like your best friend, only funnier, well-adjusted, and offering good advice. Her perspective on trauma and recovery comes from a personal place...making it real, raw, and useful. This book will leave you laughing, and better prepared to deal with life's emotional hurdles."

–Joana Emmolo, MD

"Giulia's work is incredible! The way she communicates mental health is approachable, relatable, even funny at times, and actually allows us to help ourselves. I can't recommend her work highly enough!"

–Alex Weber

"Giulia Preziuso is the mental health guide you have been looking for. She has studied and practiced mental health counseling for years, but more importantly she has struggled and suffered and overcome personally. Her irreverent and no-B.S. take on mental health is both refreshing and effective. Always direct, and at times laugh-out-loud funny, this book is guaranteed to enable your better mental wellness and emotional stability."

–Shawn M. Talbott, PhD, CNS, LDN, FACSM, FAIS, FACN, Chief Science Officer

"In a time when the world is tumultuous and in desperate need of intrinsic healing Giulia Preziuso's book is a brilliant powerful gift to those who are ready to address their trauma, finally alleviate it and enjoy their "Post Trauma Glow Up". The wisdom and deep down to earth tools Giulia shares are both powerful and practical allowing for for anyone who's seeking liberation from their pain and deep healing to transform successfully.

Her vivacious realness and huge heart coupled with her vast knowledge of the human psyche and biology comes through compassionately having us feeling as though we are taking a life changing journey with our wise therapist, most trusted confidant, and best friend."

–Jessica Smith, International Dating Coach and
Author of *21 Days to Feeling Gorgeous.*

Contents

Acknowledgments

I want to thank Ben Allen, my publisher, for encouraging me to write this book and "do what I always do" through a different medium. While I battled the professional wars and the COVID-19 quarantine, our pep talks restored my fight and helped me come back home to myself for this project. If this book does nothing else, the greatest return is in what it has taught me about myself.

Thanks to Jenn Collins, my editor, for your patience and understanding that I sometimes need to read and also hear you slowly say things repeatedly until we both laugh and I understand. Thank you for your encouragement during the hard times when all I wanted to do was quit. I appreciate you. To Maggie McGill Photography, Rutherford, NJ, for bringing the vision for the cover to life.

To Kevin Flynn, the genius behind @whitepeoplehumor, for being my marketing guru and guide on this journey. Thank you for caring about mental health. You are appreciated.

Special Mentions:

To Joana Emmolo, for being my friend by force and my sister by choice. For being there for me with unconditional love during each of my defining moments. You are my ride or die, my best friend. I love you. Wu-Tang forever.

Finally, to my Instagram family, especially the #SelfCare-Sunday crew, for your continued love and support: thank you.

I'm grateful to my parents for being the vehicles of my existence.
And I'm so grateful for my therapist, Harriet Leventhal,
for teaching me that it could be a meaningful one.
And thank you, God, for knowing it would be purposeful.

[1]*I am still learning how to go back and reread my own chapters without feeling like I want to set all of my pages on fire.*
~ E.V. Rogina ~

Introduction

The inspiration for writing this book came from the thousands of messages I've received throughout seven years (and counting) of running a mental health meme page on Instagram. The page is called @MyDefiningMoment, and this book wouldn't exist without it. I started the page while I was in graduate school, but with no real purpose behind it other than to spread some words of encouragement—and maybe just help one person feel better on any given day. I had no idea it would turn into such an impactful page, with over 150,000 loyal followers as of writing this. Every day, I answer questions related to depression, anxiety, self-worth, trauma, raising kids, being married, being single, and surviving toxic, abusive relationships. Many of you reading this have already interacted with me through that page, and your stories of resilience and supportive messages of encouragement compelled me to write this book. The idea of providing psycho-educational captions to improve your mental health coupled with inappropriate memes to make you laugh has been a well-received concept, and I thank you for embracing it.

The experience of writing a book has challenged me intellectually—and very much so emotionally, as well. I wrote this

1 E.V. Rogina Poetry

book during the 2020 pandemic while in quarantine from the novel coronavirus, COVID-19. Since it had long been a goal, I thought writing a book would be a good use of my free time, but underestimated the struggle of adjusting to life in quarantine. And I did struggle, a lot. I struggled with the ideas, the content, my abilities, and the outlines; I tore up pages, cried, and vowed to give up forever . . . only to inevitably sit back down again until I finished it. In this book, I've attempted to help readers understand all aspects of mental health that will be most useful in achieving emotional stability and mental wellness.

So, how did I get here to the point where I'm offering this book to you in hopes of enabling better mental wellness and emotional stability? After completing graduate school and all of the post-graduate clinical requirements associated with it, I went into private practice, and Defining Moments, LLC got a brand-new identity; but that wasn't actually the start of all this. Defining Moments was founded in 2007, seven years before I knew I would be counseling and coaching others; it was birthed after one of my most significant, defining milestones in life, which was losing 125 pounds in 10 months—with no surgery, no detox teas, and no staples. The achievement came through hard work, dedication, commitment, and consistency. It was February 8, 2009, when three of my best childhood friends and I were sitting around complaining about being fat while eating McDonald's #1 supersize value meals. The truth is, we were not just fat; we were morbidly obese, as my doctor put it. At my heaviest, I weighed 265 pounds—a size 28 in women's clothing—and I was emotionally tormented by the pain that comes with obesity.

I'll get to the part when I took back my life and how you can do the same, but first, I want to share a little more of my story, so stick with me. My struggle with obesity started as far back as I can remember. In kindergarten, I was 90 pounds and very aware of how different I looked from everyone else. I remember lining up in the school hallway to get weighed in by the nurse—she took one look at me in my gray and pink jogging suit and shook her head. "You're too big, honey," she said. She wasn't the only one to make comments, and relentless teasing combined with the persistent rejection I felt from peers caused me to develop significant mental health problems at an early age.

In addition to being morbidly obese, I grew up in the Riverside section of a struggling, inner-city portion of Paterson, New Jersey, and am the first American born of Italian immigrants. Fitting in would always prove to be a challenge for me, and I often felt alone. While I was growing up, my parents worked around the clock to provide for my material needs, neither one of them being equipped to provide emotional support for what I was going through. But the more depressed I became, the worse my behaviors were. I struggled most with interpersonal relationships—first with making friends, and later with having healthy romantic relationships, as well as generally getting along with others. High school was easily the most difficult period of my life for a variety of reasons. I was sent to an all-girls Catholic high school in the upper-crust suburbs of a town I didn't feel I belonged in. I felt like an outsider and began to turn inward on myself. But to turn inward is to isolate, be depressed, be angry, and lash out. For me, it meant carrying myself like someone who hated herself. As I got older and the behaviors worsened, so did the consequences.

In the end, I had my fair share of legal problems for delinquent behaviors and fighting until my 20s came, and then I realized I needed to rethink the life I was living and the path I was headed down. After experiencing more serious legal issues, it was time for me to face my demons. As part of my deal, I would see a psychiatrist, and he prescribed some meds and told me to come back in 30 days. At that time, there was no way in hell that I was taking medication—the old school Italian culture had done a fine job of ensuring I had no trust in medicine or doctors. I threw them in the trash and decided it was time to change my lifestyle instead.

After that night of binging on junk food with my friends, I woke up on February 9, 2009 and went for a walk around the block. It was all I could do, at that size, without losing my breath and fighting for my life to make it back up the hill on East 18th Street. There was no way I was going to the gym, either; it felt far too humiliating to show up and work out around other people. But I promised myself that I would walk a little further every day . . . and I did. I even walked in the rain, sleet, snow, or on ice. Nothing could stop me. In addition to walking, I cleaned up my diet and cut carbs and sugar, following the popular low-carb diet of the time. I worked up to walking five miles a day, seven days a week, and with my new low-carb lifestyle, I lost 75 pounds in the first three months, and after 10 months, 125 pounds was gone!

Everyone was amazed, and some even thought I was on drugs. The boys on the block would say, "Damn! Have you seen Giulia!? She looks like she's on that crackhead diet!" I still laugh when I tell that story. I felt so good—amazing, like a brand-new person—and I never even needed to take those stupid pills.

Unfortunately, losing weight did not cure my depression or anxiety; in fact, if anything, my symptoms worsened over time, and eventually, I had to take the stupid pills I'd refused. I'd gained confidence that they worked when you were willing to do the accompanying work in therapy, and that was my next move. This was the most important move for me—the decision to find a therapist.

By this time, I had read enough self-help books to believe that therapy would be helpful. Although I knew I would be shamed for my decision (because in my culture, therapy is for crazy people), I did it anyway. Despite that pain, I have no regrets. I've been fortunate to have found and connected so intimately with a skilled helper named Harriet. My relationship with her taught me how to truly trust another human being. It taught me, for the first time in my life, to understand what intimacy in a relationship looks like and the gift of unconditional love.

If you've followed me on Instagram, then you have seen and heard me say countless times that there is no intimacy without vulnerability and that the therapeutic setting will make you feel so vulnerable that you'll feel naked. With every story I told, with each moment when she held my darkness in sacred space, I was able to peel away the layers, heal, access the best versions of me, and develop a much-needed relationship with myself. Today, I jokingly say that I continue to see my therapist because I have to keep "trust" on the payroll; that's true, but it's also because not only is she brutally honest, but she also continues to challenge me to stretch a little bit further and broaden my perspectives each session. She sees in me what I cannot see in myself, and when you know someone believes in you, it helps motivate you. Going to and staying in therapy was absolutely another defining milestone for me, as it led to my pursuit of a career in the mental health field and put me on the path to being an effective, struggle-certified clinician.

The degrees and the certifications that I've worked hard for look fabulous hanging on my walls, and yet I don't feel like my education is what certifies me to teach you. My life struggles and my understanding of human suffering are what qualify me, so that's why I like to say I'm struggle-certified and licensed.

The pain I have endured has now found purpose that allows me to relate to others in meaningful ways, helping them gather the strength they need to transform their pain into purpose. My healing and personal development journey is why I have the courage to think that I am capable of guiding any one of you. And because I've committed myself to understanding trauma, diagnosis, behaviors, cognitive distortions, attachment disorders, and dozens of healing modalities that have brought me back home to myself, I now have a template to share with others.

I've written this book in four parts. Part 1 will teach you about different types of trauma and the specific areas of your brain that are impacted. Part 2 will focus on understanding mental health from the medical, psychological-sociological, and spiritual models of mental health. Part 3 hones in on understanding attachment disorders and their impact on relationships—especially romantic ones. And finally, in Part 4, I will help you tackle the cognitive distortions that get in the way of your healing, show you how to reframe those, and will discuss other effective treatment modalities for you to consider.

The content of this book is everything I wish I'd known sooner, but found out the hard way later. My hope is that it provides you with the knowledge to give you the power and self-control you need so that you can get a grasp on your mental health and learn how to stabilize it. In addition to learning self-regulation skills, your level of self-awareness will increase, too. This will help you to identify the unhealthy patterns that were passed down to you and give you an opportunity to rebuild your sense of self, choosing what you now believe to be true. Take what's helpful and leave the rest.

Part 1:

A Closer Look at Trauma

LIFE HACK: when someone says they're struggling right now you do not have to point out that other people have it worse.

My work over the years has led me to specialize in trauma, as I believe that going back to understand the impact of your early experiences in life will help you understand why you feel the way you do today, and that this understanding may motivate you to embark on the journey of self-love and healing. In working with clients, it's become common for me to hear them minimizing their experiences. When they share their pain and trauma in life, they preface them with qualifying statements—like "This is probably going to sound stupid," "I know it could have been worse," or "I wish I could just get over it." And it's this continued minimalization of the human experience that creates lowered self-worth, including cognitive distortions that cause mental illnesses and personality disorders. Not thinking that your experiences in life are worthy of being heard creates faulty beliefs that act as hurdles in the healing process, and these faulty filters cause blockages that stall a person's ability to create a stable life worth living. People who make such comments suffer in perpetual states of mental illness, varying in degree, that interfere with their quality of life.

I have also come to realize that no one wants to be pitied and that most people cringe at the very idea of someone feeling sorry for them. What does this have to do with those statements we were just talking about? Learning the difference between sympathy and pity is important, as learning to have a little sympathy for yourself will go a long way in helping you create stability in your mental health.

Learning more about trauma, what "qualifies" as trauma, and what symptoms look like will help you see the specific areas of your life that are being impacted by your past traumas. Comprehending the areas of the brain that are impacted by traumatic incidents and how that translates into specific behaviors will also increase your understanding and allow you to reflect on yourself and your story through a new lens—one that's sympathetic and compassionate toward the self, or in other words, you.

To manage your mental health effectively, you'll need to learn the different aspects of it. I've seen that, with this level of understanding, people can truly transform their lives. When it comes to the meaning of words and knowing that understanding varies from person to person, looking at the definition is helpful. According to the Oxford dictionary, "trauma is a deeply distressing or disturbing experience. The emotional shock following a stressful event or a physical injury."[2] However, this definition does not offer us any specific examples of what qualifies as "trauma." So we have to turn to the Diagnostic and Statistical Manual of Mental Disorders, Fifth Edition (DSM-5) for additional explanation. The DSM-5 is the reference book that helps clinicians like me provide people with diagnoses that both validate and create an understanding of a person's painful thoughts, behaviors, and mental health concerns. In the DSM's entry for post-traumatic stress disorder (PTSD), we learn that "trauma can be the result of experiencing firsthand, witnessing, or learning about a traumatic incident" which means that such an incident doesn't have to happen directly to you for you to be traumatized by it (DSM-5, 2013) . This makes trauma a subjective experience, and how a person feels is not judged or ranked in order to minimize or disqualify their experience.

If you've been battling anxiety and depression for as long as you can remember, then it's time to start reflecting on your experiences overall to determine what went wrong and then learn how to process that part of yourself appropriately so that you can ultimately heal. In addition to anxiety and depression, various symptoms are commonly reported as a reaction to trauma, regardless of the type of trauma experienced. Here, it's important to note that while I understand trauma to be a permanent injury to the brain that has no

2 Oxford Dictionary

permanent cure, I can teach you how to align your mind and body together—bringing them back into a regulated state, which makes symptoms more manageable and, for some people, eliminates symptoms entirely for extended periods of time. When symptoms persist for more than a month, the condition is considered *pathological*, which means it is time to get some help. The most commonly reported symptoms of trauma are: anxiety, irritability, mood swings, numbness, detachment, guilt, shame, anger, insomnia, restlessness, sadness, tearfulness, confusion, catatonia, withdrawal, isolation, fear, hypervigilance, nightmares, fatigue, substance abuse, avoidance, rage, flashbacks, disassociation, trust issues, abandonment, codependency, people-pleasing, low self-worth, eating disorders, body dysmorphia, binge eating, nausea, GI disturbances, chronic pain, behavioral outbursts, poor concentration, easily distractable, forgetfulness, loss of work, drop in grades, financial troubles, legal trouble, apathy, despair, distress, depression, cognitive distortions, loss of belief in anything, homicidal ideation, and suicidal ideation. Some people experience all of the symptoms that are listed above, while others have only some.

Anyone trying to cope with these distressing symptoms without the skills to manage them will spiral down some dark rabbit holes. In that darkness is a lot of pain, too, and humans will generally do anything to escape it. The most common way of escaping is through numbing oneself via substances, sex, porn, video games, food, etc. According to the Substance Abuse and Mental Health Services Administration

(SAMHSA), 75 percent of men and women in substance abuse treatment centers report histories of abuse and trauma; 97 percent of homeless women with mental illnesses report severe physical or sexual abuse; and 12–34 percent of individuals in substance abuse treatment centers have PTSD. About one-third of people exposed to trauma develop PTSD, and while men report a higher incidence of trauma, women are more likely to develop PTSD.[3] These statistics make complete sense because when you are in so much emotional pain as trauma entails, you will look for any way possible to soothe it, and when your soothing skills are limited, then your choices are as well. We need to comfort ourselves when we're in distress, but some of the choices we've been taught for feeling better end up doing us more harm than good. By learning self-love, you will also make wiser decisions when choosing how to soothe and what to do.

Talking about trauma and observing people's reactions to the word "trauma" have taught me that it is uncomfortable and confusing for many people. This is mostly because they do not feel that they've earned the word "trauma" describing their experience in life—at least, not when compared to others who have "had it much worse." Some people have been conditioned to believe that what happened to them was not that big of a deal, and when we are forced to compare our

3 Aurelie Tinland, Laurent Boyer, Sandrine Loubière, Tim Greacen, Vincent Girard, Mohamed Boucekine, Guillaume Fond, Pascal Asquier. Victimization and posttraumatic stress disorder in homeless women with mental illnes are associated with dpression, suicide and quality of life, (2018).

experiences to those of others, we create an artificial ranking system that qualifies or disqualifies a person's experience with trauma. Some trauma is active, and some is passive, and since not all trauma leads to disorders, a person can quickly be made to feel insignificant since it appears that they're fine after the fact. Yet, appearing to be fine when you're not is a skill or defense mechanism that can protect you from having a complete mental breakdown. Wearing a mask isn't anything new for many of you reading this, I know, as you've been putting one on for years to hide your mental illness from others.

What Is Trauma?

There are three different types of trauma: acute, chronic, and complex. *Acute trauma* stems from one single incident, such as a car accident, divorce, being robbed, being sexually assaulted, being in school during a shooting, or watching the world fall apart during a pandemic. When trauma is repeated over a prolonged period of time, it is referred to as *chronic trauma.* Chronic trauma is what affects the child who is abused for years at the hands of a parent, a neighbor, or a priest. It comes from a man or woman surviving a dysfunctional relationship and being emotionally or physically abused. Lastly, when a multitude of different traumas occur separately or at the same time, clinical professionals refer to the trauma as *complex trauma.* Complex trauma describes the experience of the abused child who then unconsciously enters one abusive relationship after another as an adult. For instance, complex trauma is also the intergenerational pain that comes from poverty and the dire living conditions of an unseen population. Complex trauma is the experience of serving your country, witnessing the atrocities of war, and coming home to infidelity and a broken home.

Now, here's where I want you to start engaging with this book and your own healing.

When you begin reflecting on those moments in life that have felt traumatic to you, you may become flooded with uncomfortable emotions. Write down those traumas. What are the feelings? Write those down, too. Pay attention to your body when you stumble upon an uncomfortable memory and the feelings that it brings along with it. Where in your body do you feel it? Write that down. Pay attention to your immediate reaction in the moment—are you trying to escape by distracting yourself with something else? Escaping discomfort is a very normal response. Here, you're trying to raise your level of awareness by observing yourself feeling this way, engaging through reflection. Being more attuned to your body will help you self-regulate, choosing effective skills for regulating your emotions by identifying where you feel them in your body.

Emotion regulation skills help us to stay present, even when it's not pleasant. The past can very much become a part of the present, and sadly, it has the power to negatively color your future, too. Experiencing trauma at an early age may lead to developmental deficits such as being emotionally unavailable and thus result in trouble in adult relationships, both personally and professionally. People with unresolved trauma histories often struggle with their mental health, have symptoms of anxiety and depression, and cannot maintain the consistency needed for taking care of themselves, speaking up for themselves, or creating the life they want to see themselves lead. They have a heightened sense of fear that prevents them from trying new things unless they feel fully capable, and they are also more likely to isolate and turn to substances to numb pain. This potential pattern is the danger of telling yourself or anyone else to just "get over it" when it comes to trauma. Traumatic experiences very much shape who we become and our perception of life.

When people come into the therapeutic process and begin participating in treatment, they develop sympathy for themselves, and that allows for self-love and a new sense of responsibility, which is needed for them to protect their emotional state and thus feel mentally well. This sense of inner stability helps them to visualize and create the best possible future for themselves. They have recognized, validated, and honored the pain of their past selves caused by traumatic incidents. They have taken the time to review their trauma timelines, intentionally seeking out their wounded parts and allowing themselves—in the present moment—to validate those parts of their identity, reframing negative feelings without judgment or criticism. A lens of compassion allows each wounded part of oneself to be carefully considered, understood, and heard. You become for yourself the nurturing, attentive, and loving adult, parent, and caretaker you needed.

One of the most loving things you can do for yourself is to

honor what has happened and then use that pain as a catalyst for a future worth living, where you are taking care of yourself, being fully present, and participating in the moment. Staying in the present moment is hard work—especially when the present is sometimes not very pleasant, and so it would be completely normal to want to check out and numb yourself with a bottle of wine, TV, drugs, or anything else that would take the hurt away. Because who wants to sit with pain? No one does, but the truth is that learning to sit with pain is the only way to see yourself through to the other side.

Be willing to learn how to identify and name distressing feelings which will allow you to process them in a healthy manner after you learn the techniques you can apply. Sadly, emotion regulation, feelings, and mental health aren't as important in school as core math.

Understanding Trauma and Our Brains:

Understanding your amazing brain and its impact on your body will be helpful to healing and feeling emotionally well. Having a working knowledge of how you tick helps you to use the right technique to regulate yourself. You can help ease the symptoms you experience and feel empowered rather than stuck. Too often, people will write themselves off and believe that the symptoms they experience are what they are—and there's no changing them. This is self-judgment speaking, and it's useless . . . especially if you want to improve your mental health.

Understanding how your human brain functions is important because no matter how you feel about the severity of a circumstance, your brain still responds the same way as another person's brain when confronted with an entirely different experience. With over seven billion people on earth, we all have the same human brain that mostly works the same way. When we validate one another's traumatic experiences instead of ranking them, we also stop viewing those experiences as weaknesses, character defects, or vests of shame, all of which contribute to poor mental health. What happened to you does not make you weak, bad, or whatever negative label you've attached to yourself. And denying yourself the experience of processing the trauma altogether minimizes you as a person. We spend so much time looking for our differences, but taking a moment to look at the biological responses built into our shared brain structure and function may help us validate each other more readily.

Understanding our complex brains and how they respond

to stimuli creates a shared experience when it comes to feeling pain—even if its cause differs. Trauma affects specific areas of your brain, which then contribute to behavioral changes, cognitive distortions, malignant personality traits, and mental illnesses. The beautiful brain has so many amazing parts, though, and for the purpose of understanding how active and passive trauma impact it, we will start here by learning about the hippocampus, the amygdala, the different parts of the cortex, and the brainstem.

Your *brainstem*'s function is mostly involved with basic life needs such as breathing, simple movements, consciousness, temperature regulation, and swallowing and processing food. The brainstem builds the highway to the cortex and sends it messages about food needs, resting, and water intake, and then the manager for the cortex carries those functions out. The cortex is always busy scanning the external environment while the brainstem monitors the internal environment. It will send messages about nausea, choking, shortness of breath, etc. to the cortex, which then sends the appropriate behaviors out. During acute trauma, the brainstem reacts by activating the flight, fight, freeze, or fawn response. The fawn response is the equivalent of playing dead; people are able to disconnect from themselves via dissociation, their breathing and metabolism slow down, and they become very still. This response helps us to survive when the other responses can't be accessed. Some people remain in these active states, unable to fully participate in their lives, which causes interpersonal problems and mental illness.

Deeply embedded in the brain's temporal lobe is the *hippocampus*; this is an important part of the limbic system, which is the region of your brain that regulates motivation, emotion, learning, and memory. This is also the place where the stress hormone *cortisol* is produced and regulated. Cortisol is a hormone secreted when the body is under stress, and excess cortisol levels contribute to weight gain, increased inflammatory pain, higher blood pressure, and heart disease. Trauma causes excess cortisol to be secreted, and until the trauma is resolved, it has the power to continue to hurt you not just emotionally, but physically as well. While the hippocampus is busy regulating emotions and secreting stress hormones, the *amygdala* is responsible for detecting fear and keeping you safe.

The amygdala is your internal security system, and its other core function is to process emotions and react to stimuli. This processing center is hooked up to receive incoming messages, and then the way we process those messages comes from our individual senses and intuition. Trauma can damage the amygdala, getting it stuck in a state of fear and then making it challenging to trust your intuition. The term "amygdala hijack"[4] may come into play, and hypervigilance or being easily startled are common traumatic responses. To help give you a visual, I like to think of a panic button when referring to the amygdala. For those who've endured a traumatic incident, think about that button as being stuck in the

---

4 The term "amygdala hijack" was created by psychologist Daniel Goldman in his book *Emotional Intelligence: Why It Matters More Than IQ*.

paused position, creating inappropriate responses to external stimuli. Imagine you're grabbing something from the refrigerator when someone walks up behind you and puts their hand on your back—you jump up and hit your head on the inside of the fridge, which would be an inappropriate startle response to the present moment. Trauma therapy helps to slow down reaction times so that a person can respond to a stimulus in appropriate ways and stop reacting. We can heal the amygdala and stabilize it by using strategies that employ your body's ability to regulate itself (like focusing on your breathing, learning progressive muscle relaxation techniques, and exercise, as all of these options are valuable amygdala-soothing tools).

Chronic stress, like trauma, is also responsible for a dysregulated amygdala. Stress produces anxiety and ruminating thoughts, which causes this control center in the brain to become overactive. And while this part of the brain is in overdrive, other areas of your brain that help with regulation also become impaired. The amygdala being paralyzed by a constant fear of impending doom causes direct deficits in your brain's overall functioning. When we as a society were responsible for hunting and gathering for survival, the amygdala's flight or fight response was incredibly useful. Even though we've evolved and are mostly safe today, that part of our brain continues to respond quickly to perceived threats, which causes our bodies to respond just as they were designed to do. When faced with a perceived threat, your heart will race, and you may start to sweat as adrenaline is released and your body prepares you to fight or take flight. There are other responses to this reaction, too, but for now, we will focus on the flight or fight response.

With the release of adrenaline (epinephrine), your amygdala sends a message to your cortex, which is the emotional manager, and tells it to shut down. The shutting down of the cortex means that you can't think clearly, and while this is going on, your body releases more of that stress hormone, cortisol. Cortisol then makes problem-solving and concentration impossible, and anyone in this position becomes less human and more animal.

What we have to understand is that sometimes our perceived threats are not threats at all. While we cannot predict everything that could possibly happen, there are some areas of life and experiences with certain people that have predictable patterns. Paying attention to these predictable patterns will help you to stay in control and deploy emotion-regulation techniques that thwart potential amygdala hijackings.

The next section of the brain we will examine is that manager or the *prefrontal cortex.* This part of your brain is located behind your forehead and is also known as the manager of executive functioning skills. As the manager, it is responsible for organization, planning, emotion regulation, consequences, and personality development. Its development begins in adolescence, then peaks in the teens, and completes its journey at around age 25. Understanding this area of the brain can help us empathize with teenagers a little more, as this can be an extremely emotionally challenging time for them, with the brain's developmental progression making it easy for us to blame them as people versus considering where they are in this time of crucial brain development. As the brain's network of neurons develops more synapses, an individual learns more complex skills, so while they may understand basic theories without being able to make complete connections, execution is challenging. During this time, using contemptuous words like "stupid" is incredibly damaging to the underdeveloped brain because the individual can't yet understand that mistakes will happen, as the highways of the brain are under construction. As a result, a person instead begins to think that there's something fundamentally wrong with them, thus birthing a negative inner critic. Being called names during critical brain development is demoralizing and also creates a trauma response for the brain; stress hormones are secreted, the panic button is activated, so behaviors become unpredictable. When such negative messages come from primary caretakers, they do the most damage. We have an internal desire to belong to our tribe, and so when we're rejected, that pain is as severe as if we were being whipped with a belt.

The manager is learning executive functioning skills that include your ability to focus and concentrate, as well as your being able to predict the consequences of your actions or anticipating events in your environment. Growing up in an unpredictable environment causes the brain to have a hard time mastering this skillset, as not knowing what you're going to experience causes the panic button to activate. All this contributes to the arrested development of impulse control and your ability to regulate yourself emotionally. This imbalance can look like fits of rage, losing your temper, and being short-fused. The last of the executive functioning skills being developed during this time is your ability to coordinate and adjust complex behaviors. It's knowing that you can't do B until you complete A, so although—in theory—you may feel that you or someone else should know better than to do something, the theory cannot be put into practice until the highways between these important areas of the brain are built.

Because learning how emotion regulation works is so important, looking into the prefrontal cortex a little more deeply will help you understand why you feel the way you do. It can be broken down into three parts, according to the functions they serve.

The *medial prefrontal cortex*, which controls thoughts and motivation, helps us to start and complete tasks. Any impairment to this part of the brain will create a person who feels apathetic and does not care about anything, as they are easily frustrated with their inability to focus and concentrate, which leads to poor self-esteem and contributes to learning disabilities.

Next, we have the *orbital prefrontal cortex*, which also helps with emotional regulation and impulse control. Deficits here will produce a person who behaves inappropriately where the societal norm is expected. It presents as increased agitation, anger, irritability, and poor distress tolerance skills, or no self-control. Delayed gratification is also a skill of the orbital prefrontal cortex. One study with children asked whether they would prefer to have one piece of candy immediately or wait an hour and receive two; the study showed that damage to this part of the cortex translated into an understanding of children requiring immediate gratification or none at all. So, how does this area get damaged? It can be damaged through physical harm like head injuries, loss of consciousness, or seizures, as they produce lesions or damage to this area. There is one famous case of a man named Phineas Gage who had an iron rod blown through his head, directly injuring his orbital prefrontal cortex and subsequently causing significant changes to his personality. Emotional trauma has the ability to create lesions here, too. Emotional trauma first impacts the amygdala, which senses the negative emotion, and then impacts the cortex, which should be able to rationalize and diffuse it. Emotional trauma interrupts that flow of information just like a rod to the skull. We can't just get over the things that have happened in life without fully processing them and healing because these traumas cause the brain to function in ways that make the here and now impossible to navigate, as well as causing declines in mental health.

The last part of this impressive manager of your brain is called the *lateral prefrontal cortex* and is responsible for planning, organization, and execution. Thinking again of those teenagers, who often forget things or have missing or incomplete homework and are otherwise smart, we can see that they are actually suffering from the ongoing construction of the highway development between regions of their brains. It's not that they are deliberately failing to follow through on instructions. Such failures are as distressing for them to experience as they are for a caretaker or teacher dealing with the repercussions. You will ask them, "Why did you do that? What were you thinking!?" And nine times out of ten, they will respond with "I don't know." And that is the truth, as they really don't know because the brain synapses have not been built yet. Providing a patient environment during this crucial developmental time will help a growing child learn to be patient with themselves. We can use those moments as opportunities to teach organization or other executive functioning skills, keeping in mind that the brain learns through repetition. Repeat positive behavior daily until it becomes the new norm for behavior.

One more important function of the prefrontal cortex to mention is its ability to understand empathy and compassion. Empathy is an important part of how we relate to others; some people will have super empathic skills while others have seemingly none. Empathy is the ability to correctly interpret the feelings of another and put yourself in their shoes; empathy then triggers compassion or a desire to help. Being raised in a home where emotions were not validated makes it challenging for a child to recognize emotions in others if their own emotions were not validated or recognized. While we know that empathy is innate, it is also very much conditioned by our environment and our life experiences. People who lack empathy also end up lacking compassion—not only toward others, sadly, but also toward themselves, as they've never been taught how to identify and then express their emotions, which causes them to be disconnected from others and themselves. On a side note, having this understanding, empathy or sympathy for why someone behaves the way they do, is not permission to ever excuse, justify, or tolerate toxic behaviors.

Modeling and Emotional Intelligence

Janet Forklift
@janetforklift

Therapist: "Have you ever considered that you use your appearance to push people away?"

Me: *Wearing a shirt that says DON'T FUCKING TALK TO ME* "Nah...I still think it has to do with my parents."

It is believed that our personalities are fixed by the age of three, and while those early years are important in shaping who we are, you also must take comfort in your brain's continued ability to identify poor behaviors and learn new ones. Our early years are important partly because there's no language development at that point, and so, as a child, your learning is based on your senses—everything you see, hear, smell, touch, and taste. Your senses are so incredibly powerful; they can be used to help ground yourself and control your emotions. Emotions engage the use of our senses, which we learn to access as soon as we were born, and they provide us with an incredible amount of information. Some parents make the mistake of telling themselves that their child doesn't understand what's going on because they can't speak, but children are perceptive and can pick up on every cue in their environment. A child understands tone, inflection, facial expression, and energy, and will begin to mirror it all, good or bad. Frustration tolerance is taught through non-verbal cues, as well so if you're angry with your partner and, instead of yelling, you slam doors, break things, or emote frustration in any other physical way, your non-verbal child learns those ways, too. This self-examination of non-verbal cues is a hard thing to look at, but also critical if you want to raise emotionally intelligent and mentally well humans. Learning to manage your own emotions can help you to connect and be attuned to your child's emotional needs.

Emotional intelligence (EQ) has been widely researched and taught in corporate institutions, with some focus being put on it in educational institutions as well, though not enough. Your EQ impacts your interpersonal skills and functioning. Interpersonal skills are also referred to as people skills, and they can be crucial to your educational and professional success. Being able to interact and communicate appropriately within the context of social norms and expectations is an important skill. If your boss makes you angry, flying off the handle and getting in their face will not yield a positive response. Emotion regulation and self-control are taught both directly and indirectly by our early caretakers and role models. If you have emotionally inflamed caretakers who react to stress with yelling, hitting, or other types of destructive behavior, you are more likely to model that same behavior, at least until you enter a school where it will no longer be acceptable, and you'll face educational consequences, and as you age, worse yet, legal consequences.

Interpersonal skills are also called social skills when referring to childhood development, and they vary depending on different social settings. In a school setting, children are expected to learn how to share, collaborate with others, listen to directions, follow directions, have manners, maintain eye contact, and respect the personal boundaries of others. A child who lives in an abusive environment that doesn't show respect for personal boundaries will have a harder time in that area of development. While teachers are charged with teaching social skills, these skills always start at home. And beyond school, the parent is then responsible for modeling and reinforcing what is being taught at school. What if the caretaker is a substance abuser or an alcoholic wrapped up in their disease? The child coming home to an unpredictable environment will now develop that panic button problem early on because they're not safe with the people in charge of keeping them safe. This child then grows into an adult with significantly arrested emotional development, which then impedes their interpersonal skills in the workplace and in relationships.

Interpersonal skills involve your ability to communicate

effectively in both verbal and non-verbal ways. These skills are also referred to as meta-communication when describing non-verbal communication—or everything you say without opening your mouth. Eye contact and body language communicate emotions without saying a word, and mastery in these areas improves all relationships. Related skills learned via similar development involve listening, problem-solving, decision-making, and assertiveness.

Self-Exploration Exercise:

Using visualization techniques, imagine coaching your inner child-like self through some of the traumatic experiences you've endured. How would you speak to that child today? Would you yell at them? Would you tell them that they're worthless or stupid? What would you say? Be loving. Just try it.

What Happened That Makes Me Act This Way?

People feel a great deal of distress when their emotions

are out of control and their mental health is suffering. Understanding what makes you think and act the way you do helps you to identify areas that need your compassion, love, and attention. Were you abused as a child? Raised in a dysfunctional home? Bullied? All of this will affect you later in life.

Abuse is another word that varies in definition and experience depending on the person who's experienced it. Child abuse is when a parent or caretaker directly or indirectly causes emotional or physical harm or causes some risk of harm to a child. There are many forms of child abuse, including neglect, physical abuse, sexual abuse, emotional abuse, and exploitation. Talking about this is not intended to villainize your parents or shift the blame for your life onto them, either; it is meant for you to understand why your life is not working for you right now. Understanding why something is going wrong helps you sympathize with yourself, and when you can feel compassion, you can feel love. People who genuinely love themselves create lives they love, too. When you connect with wounded parts of yourself, you are given an opportunity to re-parent them as the loving adult you are capable of being today.

Child abuse is an ongoing problem in our world, as it continues to remain hidden in dysfunctional families that encourage secrets, and maintaining their socially acceptable images has a tremendous impact on mental health. Here are just a few startling facts about child abuse:

1. Approximately five children die every day because of child abuse. (Childhelp, 2015)
2. One out of three girls and one out of five boys will

be sexually abused before they reach the age of 18. (Center, 2014)

3. Ninety percent of child sexual abuse victims know their predator in some way, and 68 percent are abused by family members. (US Department of Justice, 2014)
4. In the United States alone, more than four children die from child abuse and neglect every day; 70 percent of them are under the age of three. (Horizon, 2015)
5. Every year, 2.9 million cases of child abuse are reported in the United States. (Horizon, 2015)
6. Children who experience child abuse and neglect are 59 percent more likely to be arrested as a juvenile, 20 percent more likely to be arrested as an adult, and 30 percent more likely to commit a violent crime. (Horizon, 2015)
7. Eighty percent of 21-year-olds who were abused as children meet the criteria for at least one psychological disorder. (Horizon, 2015)
8. Fourteen percent of all men and 36 percent of all women in prison were abused as children. (Horizon, 2015)
9. Abused children are less likely to practice safe sex, putting them at higher risk for STDs, and they are also 25 percent more likely to experience teen pregnancy. (Silverman, 1996)
10. Children who are exposed to abuse and trauma may

> develop what is called a heightened stress response. This compromises their ability to regulate their emotions and leads to sleep difficulties and lower immune function while also increasing the risk of physical illnesses throughout adulthood. (US Department of Justice, 2014)

Surviving child abuse can make imagining a better life impossible when you've been dealt such a losing hand of one trauma after another. It's important to keep in mind that when you lose a hand, the deck will eventually be reshuffled, and you'll get another try. You will have as many tries as necessary. Not having caretakers to keep you safe as a child creates a deep sense of emptiness inside, but you are also equipped with everything you need to fill that void in meaningful ways. Continue working to develop self-compassion and self-love so that you can begin engaging in the self-care required for a healthy life. Once you create compassion toward your self-worth, your sense of self-value will also increase, and if you can recognize it in yourself, you will be able to extend it to others, too. Being better humans both to ourselves and to others is always a good idea in this often-cruel world.

Maybe there was no child abuse in your upbringing, but then when you got to school, the bullying began. Kids get picked on for nearly any reason at all, but these bullies picked on your physical appearance. They called you fat, called your ears too big, or told you that you had a funny walk, so every day of school was filled with anxiety and fear of another day facing humiliation and embarrassment. In 2021, such bullying has been taken to an even grosser sociopathic level by recording bullying events and then sharing them on social media platforms. Imagine all of this happening to you and then not having a safe place to go home to; imagine that home is just like school, and the only people you thought you could trust torment you, as well.

What's a kid to do in these circumstances? Most of them will turn inward and breathe life into a negative inner voice that will grow more powerful with every criticism, destroying mental health and replacing it with self-hatred. They'll start to withdraw and isolate; self-harm usually begins here to release some of the internal pain. Victims of such circumstances will do whatever it takes to release the pain and turn to others who have also been rejected to create a tribe of acceptance. Substance abuse becomes acceptable, so using alcohol, marijuana, or whatever they can get their hands on becomes the preferred coping mechanism. Nothing matters anymore because they don't feel like they matter, and so they treat themselves accordingly.

Bullying that occurs during puberty creates long-lasting mental health problems. Puberty is defined as the time during which adolescents reach sexual maturity and become capable of reproduction. You may be "capable of reproduction," but maybe no one has bothered to explain to you what the hell is going on in your body. For girls, you grow breasts (or maybe you don't), and your hips get wider to prepare for the fetus you might someday carry; you're fully capable of doing that right now, even though you've just recently learned how to tie your shoes and still can't make eye contact with people.

Boy or girl, your face gets oily, and acne develops; your anxiety gets worse because now there are more things for people to make fun of you for. You feel depressed and rejected like an outcast, so you cling to anything that provides comfort. You've learned to live with a very loose definition of comfort, so anything will work as long as it's something. Common problems that teenagers face today include self-esteem and body image issues, as well as bullying, depression, technology addiction, substance abuse, underage sex, teenage pregnancy, peer pressure, acceptance and rejection, and even legal problems. It's sad to see how often teenagers are dismissed because they don't have any "real problems"—often enough, they have all of the real problems that adults have.

The brain learns in several ways, including repetition, what it sees and what happens to it, coding templates for the future and repeating patterns. When there's dysfunctional programming in the family, then you're also being unconsciously groomed to experience toxic relationships later. You don't know what red flags are because you've only ever seen red, and the code that was programmed is simple but destructive: "The worse I treat you, the more I love you—because I do it for you, but because you made me do it, it's your fault." Early in bad relationships, you'll be less likely to leave because you've learned to tolerate anything, and there's nothing to go home to, so now you tell yourself you have to make it work somehow, some way. At this point in your emotional development, there is a strong pull toward bonding with another because the ideas of creating something better start to surface as well. You believe you'll do a better job, so you start running toward creating a new life for yourself with someone else by your side instead of learning how to stand on your own two feet by yourself first.

It's a matter of bad programming and repeating patterns.

Say you went off to college, got a job, joined the military, or did whatever was necessary to get out of your dysfunctional family. But you still don't feel good about yourself, and you're still trying to define your identity. Exploring identity is another impactful part of development that affects your mental health as it brings lots of opportunities for poor decisions. Those decisions potentially contribute to making you feel worse about yourself. When you're taught to "just get over it," you internalize your mistakes instead of forgiving yourself. Forgiveness for mistakes is not easily accessible in dysfunctional families.

For those still at home right now, who are completely dependent and unable to move out on your own yet, it's a matter of doing the work of learning how to take care of yourself. You also need to stay focused on your schoolwork; education is your ticket out of there. There's access to so much free knowledge, including support groups and online communities, so it's important that you don't buy into the idea that this life you're living is as good as it gets. If you want more for yourself and the circumstances that you've been dealt, try to find work with benefits so you can afford to go to therapy. It's also important to resist the programming you may have received around therapy and it being for "crazy" people; *crazy* is exactly what's going on in your brain, but that's okay. Finding a therapist who has empathy, compassion, and no judgment toward you can help you to transform your life and achieve things you could only imagine. Finding a healthy person who can teach you how to look at things differently is the only way to "get over" the traumas you've endured that have contributed to where you are today.

The danger of not allowing yourself to receive any compassionate influences is that you'll only continue to build upon and repeat bad patterns. You may find yourself in relationships that mirror the relationship your parents had. Those of you who come from divorced parents may feed into the idea of that happening in your own life and self-sabotage your relationships and trigger abandonment. If you witnessed violence in your family, you might be more tolerant of it in relationships, and you may even find yourself poking and looking for fights to trigger the behaviors that you've come to understand as love. Physical or emotional abuse is never okay, not in any relationships, ever. It's worth noting that the damage of poor programming doesn't stop with personal relationships; it also flows into the workplace. You may be surrounded by bullies as an adult, especially if you're more passive and don't know how to assert yourself. You may be afraid to speak up against poor treatment for fear of losing your job, so now the workplace is unsafe for you as well. Your workload piles up because you're the go-to person for everyone, and then you feel overwhelmed and helpless with nobody to help you. You don't know how to ask for help, and you have trouble speaking up for yourself too.

Others who have had to "just get over it" choose positions that expose them to more trauma, adding layers to the complex trauma cake. Brave men and women enter the armed forces as a way to both create a stable future for themselves *and* escape their troubled environments. They are deployed to war-savaged countries and bear witness to the most atrocious human behaviors. Some of them participate in it because they see no other options, and others because they want to, but when they come home, there's no one to talk to—making their minds another warzone. We commonly associate post-traumatic stress disorder with war veterans, but for many of them, this is not the first time that they've experienced such trauma. After completing tours in the military, many of these men and women also continue their service to our country through positions in law enforcement, which is another thankless career and will potentially lead to them being directly and/or indirectly traumatized every time they show up for work. The "just get over it" mentality trends in the first-responder community, too, making them the most vulnerable to suffering in silence.

Minimizing life's experiences makes you further and further detached from yourself and your feelings because it's a survival technique. Cutting and compartmentalizing is the only way to stop yourself from losing your mind. Every first responder I have worked with—whether military, medical, or law enforcement—has had a story that has forever changed them, a story that they will never forget, a story that feels like it comes to life every time they speak of it, over and over again whenever they tell it. What we're talking about here are essentially flashbacks, which are a common symptom of PTSD and important to understand. They are defined as "vivid, intrusive thoughts that involve reliving some aspects of a traumatic event or which make it feel as if the event is happening in the here and now." (DSM-5, 2013) They can be activated through your senses, such as with sounds or smells that connect to the original trauma, triggering a panic attack or other feelings of anxiety in the body. Survivors of sexual assault will sometimes freeze into the fetal position during a flashback, with their bodies tensing up as they recall the assault. Another will gaze out a window while they tell the story, as though they're watching it happen to someone else. The same emotional and physical experiences occur for those who suffered abuse as a child, so while we may feel like we've gotten over such a traumatic experience, the body hasn't forgotten. If we can better understand how the biological reactions we have are the same across a variety of human experiences, despite the different trauma types and degrees, we may be more willing to share our stories and seek help with our mental health.

What we don't heal from, we repeat and pass down to the next generation. When working with trauma survivors who are also parents, I've found that many of them feel a tremendous amount of guilt and fear—guilt because they've already messed up their kids in some way or fear that they will. While you will likely do a better job than what you received as a child, you are also going to print malware patterns on your children, and those will be replicated down the generations to come. Healing is the only way to stop the poison from traveling and infecting the innocent, as it breaks the chains of generational curses.

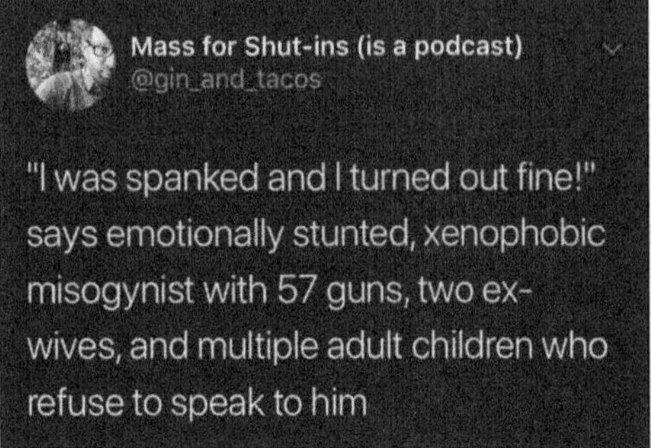

In addition to flashbacks, important feelings to elaborate on are those of emotional detachment and persistent loneliness. Severe trauma exposure in childhood also makes people more vulnerable to developing severe mental illnesses like schizophrenia. Epidemiological studies show that exposure to early stressors such as physical abuse or neglect in childhood increases the risk of developing schizophrenia. In 2012, research at the University of Liverpool found that children who experienced trauma were three times as likely to develop delusional disorders, psychosis, and schizophrenia.[5]

A client who provided me with consent to share her story talked about how, out of the blue one day while she was at work, she had a flashback to being molested as an eight-year-old child. Something about the customer she was helping triggered a memory so powerful that she fell into a deep state of mental illness and was unable to return to work for three

5 Schizophrenia Bulletin: Volume 34, Issue 3 May 2009

months. During this time, she described persistent images that attacked her as often as she blinked, and when she finally made a psychiatry appointment, she was heavily addicted to drugs and experiencing food disorders, desperate to numb her pain and stop the memories from attacking her. It was through seeking professional help that she gained an understanding of what was happening. It was comforting for her to know that what she was experiencing was normal, considering what she'd been through. Medication helped treat the panic attacks and constant anxiety, while other medications helped reduce the flashbacks, and therapy helped her learn ways to soothe herself in the moment and regulate her emotions before she could be hijacked by her mind. Soon, she was able to recognize the physical symptoms that her body sent out as warning signs of oncoming flashbacks, and those signals then caused her to use her skills to prevent the flashbacks.

Sometimes, such symptoms as these flashbacks will go away by themselves, and sometimes they never do, so learning what to do when you are triggered will help improve your quality of life. When you start peeling back the layers, you will hurt, and it will unlock new feelings that you did not know were possible, that you did not know you had—bringing days and nights of gut-wrenching sobbing, where you shed tears for all the parts of you that were hurt. That's your opportunity to get in there and fill yourself with love and compassion in your adult body, capable of soothing yourself in healthy ways.

To unlock the castle in your mind, imagine a room for

every year you've lived, each one filled with a different version of you. How would you approach two-year-old you? Or 12-year-old you? How about 16-year-old you? It's harder to face some parts than others, as some of them trip up that toxic shame because you're still busy blaming yourself for what happened. You've tried to just get over it, but it's still locked inside of you.

People who develop CPTSD (Complex PTSD) often have the same things in common—a history of child abuse and a pre-existing mental health issue likely picked up in childhood. When I ask clients to tell me how far back their depression or anxiety goes, it's not uncommon to hear that it goes as far back as they can remember. They come to me in their 60s, 70s, and 80s after having lived an entire lifetime of suffering from symptoms without any understanding of them and without much consideration or thought for themselves or their own well-being. A lack of unconditional love and support perpetuates the illnesses, as does not wanting to look at it in therapy. They take medication after medication that does not work because they can't work—at least, not on their own; we can't pretend that you can take a magic pill and it can cure all of these distressing feelings. But when everything you try fails, living becomes intolerable, and so a common theme for trauma survivors is chronic suicidality. For many clients, knowing that this is a common symptom helps them feel less afraid and more able to manage symptoms.

Many of you feel like you've tried everything and nothing will work, but the mere fact that you've picked up this book tells me that you still want to try. Trying means allowing someone to love you through the therapeutic process; this has to be someone who you can share yourself with, someone who you can give your shame to, so that you have somewhere to unpack it all and leave it all behind. This doesn't mean that you'll forget, but it does mean that you'll feel a release, and the more that you're able to let go, the more you will see that you were always worthy. You were always good enough, and you didn't deserve any of that trauma. You'll get mad, you'll cry, and every time you do, you'll feel a little bit better. You will walk on more solid ground and be ready to learn skills for the management of your symptoms as they come. You'll learn more power and self-control when you decide to *not get over it, but to get through it* because emotion regulation and mental health stability are possible.

Part 2: Understanding the Components of Mental Health

When we first learn about mental health, it's usually to understand why we're depressed or anxious. Generally, we weren't taught early on to consider, let alone include in our lives, the daily habits and routines that can help us to stay mentally well. What I've learned along the way in my own treatment, my education, and my practice has led to the development of a mental wellness template that, once created, can be applied to help us feel mentally stable on more days than not. You'll have some bad days here and there, but once you have a good grasp on your wellness plan, you'll know what to do to ensure you get yourself through those bad days. I believe that mental illness and mental wellness are states of temporary being, and people can fluctuate between them throughout their days; where they are on the spectrum of mental health is contingent on how present they are in the moment and how conscious they are of their emotional states. I also believe that a diagnosis of a mental illness should not be treated as a life sentence—symptoms will fluctuate, and you're capable of understanding and making conscious changes to help yourself get and stay mentally well. It's all about how we think about these terms and our own mental health. A diagnosis of a mental illness is given when there is social, educational, or occupational impairment causing significant distress that interferes with a person's quality of life. Mental health is explained to us through several different models, and they are all useful in their own way for helping us understand it.

In brief, mental health can be examined through medical, psychological, sociological, and/or spiritual lenses. Understanding these different models will help you to understand what has caused or is currently contributing to your poor mental health. When you can understand that, then you can plan for your future mental health and look for the areas where you have power and control to make changes. I strongly believe that being mentally well involves balance and alignment of mind, body, and spirit.

The Medical Model and a Template for Good Self-Care

[tv announcer] Are you bloated? Tired? Unable to enjoy the activities you once loved?

[me with mouthful of chips] YEAH

The medical model of mental health concludes that mental illness can be treated in the same way as a broken limb. Disorders are caused by genetics, neurotransmitters, neurophysiology, and neuroanatomy, and the model looks at the structure and functioning of the brain to find the root cause of illnesses. This approach views mental health through a lens that seeks out an organic or physical cause of illness, with it being those factors that create symptoms in a patient. Those symptoms are then classified into disorders and help medical doctors diagnose; those diagnoses then call for specific medications that help patients manage and sometimes cure their symptoms. Medications and the science of psychopharmacology are incredibly valuable, and seeing firsthand how they can improve someone's quality of life is truly remarkable.

Early on in my mental health career, I spent several years in a psychiatric setting, observing why some people got better while others never made any progress at all. I learned about their lifestyles, self-care, family history, and all of the treatments they'd tried. A common factor for the patients who didn't get better or continued to decline was poor self-care and unhealthy lifestyles. They didn't take care of themselves (or didn't do it very well, for whatever reason), lacked motivation, and couldn't maintain consistency.

Researching the medical model further, I learned about the different ways that our bodies naturally produce endorphins, which means that through intentional physical activity, we can boost our brain's production of feel-good neurotransmitters just like medications do. When anti-depressants are prescribed, their job is to help balance the brain's feel-good neurotransmitters, and those feel-good neurotransmitters are called dopamine, serotonin, and gamma-aminobutyric acid (GABA). When it comes to patients whose self-care is non-existent and whose symptoms are severe, they're not capable of doing all of the things necessary to participate in a healthy lifestyle, so medication can be useful in helping them to feel better and then be more motivated to take part in their own mental wellness. Sometimes, you know what you have to do, but you don't have the physical or emotional energy to do anything, and that's when medication becomes the most helpful; it's one of the many tools that can contribute to improved mental wellness.

If you're in a place where you feel motivated to try to improve your mental health naturally, the first prescriptive approach is to take a good look at your lifestyle. Your lifestyle includes such factors as exercise, diet, and sleep. Exercise has been shown to have tremendous benefits for a depressed mood, as it releases endorphins that trigger a positive feeling both mentally and physically. Many people report those feelings of endorphins after working out; for instance, runners refer to it as a *runner's high*. Jokingly, I like to refer to them as cocaine for your brain without all the nasty side effects—you know, like losing money, friends, self-respect, or your life!

There are so many amazing ways to implement movement into your life and gauge its efficacy when it comes to mood improvement. Always start with something you enjoy like riding a bike, going for a walk, dancing, or whatever it may be, and aim for engaging in the activity for 20 minutes a day to start, for three days a week. During the times when I was struggling the most and having a hard time motivating myself, my therapist would ask, "Can you just try for 10 minutes? How about 10 minutes in the morning and 10 minutes in the afternoon?" And that did it. "Just 10 minutes" would later become my mantra for getting through those difficult times, as 10 minutes would lead to 20, and 20 to 30, and 30 to 60. I would have to look at my clock and remind myself to turn back home because exercise became something that I could not go without doing in order to feel my best. Embracing this exercise piece of your lifestyle will also require you to redefine your relationship with exercise. For many—and I include myself in saying this—exercise is exclusively seen as a means of losing weight, and if you fail to lose weight, then you might have a completely negative perception of it. That's certainly how I saw it. But, start to reframe it as something that you *get* to do because of how good it is for your mental wellness and not just as a means to an end. That might make all the difference.

Diet is a dirty word in our culture today, as it represents a complete belief system that supports dysfunctional and unrealistic body images. Diet culture asserts that fitness is to be worshiped and equated with health and as a virtue to be attained. As a woman who struggled with and naturally beat morbid obesity, I understand the damage that this ideal can have on a person's psyche. Whenever I use the word *diet*, I use it in relation to the definition and its origin use—not as a shortcut term for a way to starve yourself in order to look good. In that spirit, I don't believe in good or bad foods, but only in food and how it makes you feel. The word "diet" comes from the Greek word "diata,"—which means *a way of life*. Finding the right diet that lends itself to you feeling your very best mentally and physically is a crucial component of mental health.

Let's look at how your primary brain communicates with your second brain, your stomach. The gut-brain axis refers to that communication in particular—and those feel-good neurotransmitters that are released when you exercise are also produced in your gut. The vast majority of serotonin is produced in the gut, and at least 50 percent of dopamine is produced there, too, making a poor diet a component that leads to mental illness. Your gut flora contains trillions of bacteria and keeping that bacteria healthy involves a diverse diet rich in probiotics, prebiotics, and phytobiotics. If your eating habits aren't stellar and you have some cleaning up to do, try adding some of the many natural supplements out there into your daily regimen to help get these benefits. Educating yourself on gut-brain axis, the microbiome, and how you can make wiser diet decisions will greatly benefit your mental health.[6]

Choosing the right foods to optimize your gut-brain axis

6 What's the state of your mental wellness? Get your personalized score, including customized recommendations, by taking this short quiz here: https://18595.amarecontent.com/
For more information on the cutting edge holistic mental optimization solutions from Amare Global, gut health and its relationship to mental wellness, and the remarkable science behind the gut-brain axis taught by world-renowned psychonutritionist Dr. Shawn Talbott, go to: https://www.definingmomentsllc.com/amare-global/

doesn't have to be complicated. There are some easy "first steps" that anyone can take, such as adding more fiber to your diet and reducing your intake of highly processed foods. Fiber is what "feeds" our microbiome bacteria—so when we eat more, we nourish our "good" bacteria (and they produce more feel-good neurotransmitters)—but when we eat processed foods that are low in fiber and high in sugar, we "starve" those good bacteria. The best way to get more fiber in your diet is to eat brightly colored fruits and vegetables, whole grains, and beans/seeds/nuts as often as possible. When you can't get your daily 5-10 servings of fruits/veggies, targeted dietary supplements can help fill the gap, and newer probiotic supplements are starting to include specific strains of bacteria that can actively reduce stress, anxiety, and depression.

Sleep is the final component in the biological model, and it has the greatest impact on mental health. Poor sleep is a common symptom of many mental illnesses, especially depression, anxiety, and ADHD. Sleep is a critical component of optimal wellness as it helps our bodies to rest and repair. When our sleep is impaired, we are often cranky, have difficulty with focus and concentration, and suffer from cognition problems. Good sleep helps our daily performance by increasing our energy levels and improving our mental functioning. A study in the *Journal of Sleep Research* looked at people's responses to emotional stimuli, and researchers concluded that a person has less emotional empathy when they have not gotten adequate sleep. (Guadagni, 2014) Adequate sleep is defined by the CDC for adults as 7–9 hours each night, with exact requirements depending on age. (Control, How much sleep do I need?, 2014) Our bodies can fall into a natural sleep-wake cycle with a little encouragement from our daily routines. A nightly bedtime routine is helpful for getting better sleep; included in that routine is going to sleep and waking up at the same time every day—including the weekends. Things like reading, stretching, meditating, hot baths or showers, and comfortable room temperatures are also good considerations to include in your routine. This next part is hard to hear, but it's also been recommended that we put our devices away a couple of hours before we go to bed, and this is due to the impact of devices on our body's melatonin production. Melatonin is a hormone that regulates the sleep-wake cycle, and it's secreted during different times of the day. The rising sun emits a blue light like the one in our devices, which tells our body to stop producing melatonin and to wake up. As the sun begins to set each day, our bodies begin producing melatonin to help us ease into a blissful sleep—which is why devices create harmful confusion, and so putting them down will help put us out. It's challenging to create boundaries around our devices since they also double as alarm clocks and radios, but if you're having trouble sleeping, it may be worth your while to invest in the stand-alone products and keep your phone on silent in another room when it's time to go to sleep.

These are the core parts of your self-care template for good mental health, but remember to redefine your relationship with them so that you can reframe these activities as something that you get to do for yourself in your own template. When I refer to creating this template, I'm talking about your lifestyle—the daily habits that you commit to and create a discipline around to stay and feel mentally well. Participating in these activities is something that you *get* to do—think of it as a privilege—and not as something that you have to do. As with anything else, taking an honest assessment of your lifestyle isn't easy, but it is necessary if you want to stay mentally well.

The Spiritual Model of Identity Formation

The spiritual model looks at the impact of religion and how a personal relationship with spirituality can contribute to psychological distress. Religious and spiritual affiliation greatly contribute to a personal sense of identity and provide a moral framework to live by. As with anything significantly influential, however, spirituality can also be used for control, dominance, or to abuse people. Any perceived breach with God or the universe creates an existential crisis for an individual, sending a person spiraling downward until they find themselves losing their sense of purpose. An absence of a relationship with a higher power may lead to questioning the purpose of life and not feeling a sense of belonging. Similarly, a close relationship with spirituality can increase a person's sense of self and have a positive impact on a person's well-being. It provides a sense of community that may not be otherwise found in their world.

Religion is powerful, and if you were raised in a strict, religious home and fell out of line with any of the rules and regulations imposed by the religion, then you also felt completely rejected when you made mistakes. This rejection causes feelings of shame, guilt, and unworthiness, which can poison your sense of self and your overall mental health over time. Some religions are so controlling that when a perfectly imperfect human being makes a mistake, the consequences are costly. For some, it costs everything—membership in one's religious organization can be lost, which equates to being disowned by one's family, and with the risks of rejection being so high, many people don't speak up when they have questions and instead, suffer in silence.

The truth is that if you are to grow in a spiritual way, you have to ask questions—because, after all, there are so many questions. What happens when we die, where we go at that point, will we ever see our loved ones again . . . the list goes on and on. When rules and regulations prevent questions and create rejection, a person falling away from believing in anything at all is common. And that existential pull will remain there until you explore it.

Consider this an invitation for you, in all autonomy, to explore any religions that interest you and take components of what brings you peace into practice in your life. When you feel unstable in life and unsure of the direction you're taking or heading toward, finding a spiritual practice will help you to feel grounded and comforted. Your relationship with spirituality will evolve as you do. Your beliefs may change over time, so it's important to remain flexible in learning, especially in something that provides a tremendous amount of peace and comfort. When you choose to believe in something bigger than yourself, it provides you with a sense of purpose and belonging, and when life deals its never-ending blows, that sense of stability is a crucial component of your mental health.

The Psycho-Social Model and Impact on Identity Development

There will be clients who have the self-care template down to a science, and yet they continue to struggle with symptoms of depression and anxiety—and have struggled in this way for as long as they can remember, creating a persistently poor mental state. The psycho-social model of mental health helps us gather more information to understand why a person is suffering. The social aspect looks at external factors that create overwhelming psychological distress—like socioeconomic status and the effects of poverty, race, and cultural components, as well as the belief systems held in place by a culture that impedes an individual from getting help. The psychological factor looks at internal components like family history, siblings, relationships with parents or primary caretakers, and sexual, physical, or emotional abuse, as well as traumatic experiences, all of which are factors contributing to a depressed mood, anxiety, or overall decline in mental health. The factors in this model contribute to personality-based disorders.

Disorders are categorized as either ego-syntonic or ego-dystonic. Ego-syntonic means that a person's behaviors, moods, values, and feelings about their problems are normal and outside of their control, usually to be blamed on external circumstances or people. This group has poor insight, does not accept ownership of their issues, nor do they take accountability for how they may be contributing to their own symptoms, poor moods, and difficult relationships. An example of this would be a person who blames their violent behavior on their father abandoning them as a child. They then get to blame their violent behavior on their father's absence forever instead of taking responsibility and learning self-control. The ego-dystonic group feels that their behaviors, moods, and feelings are unacceptable and cause them significant distress. An example would be a person who suffers from obsessive-compulsive disorder—they may have compulsive behaviors that they are repulsed by, but do not know why they are engaging in them or how to stop them; the same conclusions can be applied to those who suffer from ruminating or obsessive thoughts. The ego-syntonic group is not suffering from a mental illness, as persons in this group believe that the way they think about things is normal, so they are likely to have a personality disorder and are harder to treat—especially if they don't want to consider perspectives that might suggest how taking ownership of their lives can contribute to mental wellness. When a person is in denial of the negative impact of their thoughts and behaviors, and is treatment resistant, they may very well be diagnosed with a personality disorder.

I believe that a personality disorder is a side effect of trauma and a response to it that helps the person to cope with what they experienced; I also believe that psychotherapy can help a person identify the unhealthy parts of their personalities and intentionally change those aspects of themselves, improving their relationships and moods. Processing the circumstances that have contributed to poor mental health helps a person feel better because healing can be done in such a way that it completely changes how a person views their life. Taking the example of the violent person who blames their violent tendencies on an absent father, it's possible that showing them how to express the anger, shame, sadness, and negative emotions inside of them will allow them to reconsider whether or not they need to carry on the violence.

Personality Disorders

In the DSM-V, personalities are categorized into three distinct clusters—A, B, and C. Within these clusters are 10 distinct personality disorders. When you or someone you know has a problem that they're not willing to address, you may find yourself wanting to box them in, but as you learn about these types and clusters, resist the urge to label yourself or your loved ones with a personality disorder without getting a clinical assessment from a trained provider—because it's not fair to do otherwise. Labels also produce shame and resistance to seeking treatment. It's not uncommon to recognize traits within yourself or others in each of these personality groups and yet still not have a personality disorder.

The difference between traits and disorders involves a person's level of insight—because if you can see how you, your thinking, and your behaviors are part of the problem, interfering with your quality of life and your relationships, then you'll also be able to learn new ways of behaving, thinking, and believing. Those people in the Cluster B group, especially, don't believe that there's anything wrong with them, so they aren't actively seeking help; or, if they do seek help, they are very difficult to treat—sometimes outright treatment resistant—and may very well fire a therapist before they've had a chance to shine a light on any problematic behaviors. The point here is that if you're willing to look at the not-so-great parts of your personality and understand how they got to be a part of you so that you can address them, then you're on the right track. One of the greatest glow-ups is cleaning up toxic behaviors, attitudes, and beliefs—to glow up means recognizing your areas of opportunity and taking the steps necessary for healthy changes.

The Cluster A group is defined as the odd and eccentric group, with bizarre behavior as a core component. The related personality disorders are commonly seen in severe psychiatric conditions that I do not personally treat, so I'll just give a brief description. The personalities in this group are:

1. Schizoid personality disorder: This patient has a difficult time interpreting social cues, expressing emotion, or finding pleasure in activities. They have little desire for close relationships, including romantic, sexual, friendship, or familial.
2. Schizotypal personality disorder: These patients struggle with audible or visual hallucinations and have high levels of paranoia, which makes forming relationships difficult. They are usually eccentric in appearance and have strange ways of speaking, behaving, and dressing.
3. Paranoid personality disorder: These patients feel suspicious of others without any reason at all; they feel persecuted, targeted, and resist forming any type of meaningful relationship. (DSM-5, 2013)

The next cluster, Cluster B, is defined as the dramatic group. Many trauma survivors will display traits of this cluster, with some of them developing treatment-resistant personality disorders due to the severity of what they've endured; their personalities are a response to what happened to them. The disorders in Cluster B are histrionic, borderline, narcissistic, and antisocial. One common theme amongst the Cluster B group is erratic, dramatic, and unpredictable behavior due to low impulse control.

1. Histrionic personality disorder: This patient is marked by emotional attention-seeking behaviors and a need to be the center of attention, with a heavy emphasis on physical appearances being manipulated accordingly. There is inappropriate, provocative, and sexually seductive behavior exhibited in clothing choices that draw a lot of attention. They are shallow in their expression of emotion and tend to express themselves in big, theatrical ways. They show significant naivety, poor personal boundaries, and are easily influenced into believing that relationships are more intimate than they actually are.
2. Borderline personality disorder: Most clinicians will tell you that the borderlines are the hardest to treat and are most likely to have a poor prognosis. These patients show behavior marked by a pattern of unstable interpersonal relationships, low self-image, and high impulsivity. These patients frantically try to avoid real or imagined abandonment as they alternate between extremes of love and hate. A great book to pick up if you want to learn more about this aspect of the disorder is *I Hate You – Don't Leave Me* by Jerold J. Kreisman and Hal Straus.

These patients struggle with a sense of self and identity, with chronic feelings of emptiness. There's impulsivity in at least two of the following areas: spending, sex, substance abuse, reckless driving, and/or binge eating. There is also recurrent suicidal behavior, threats, or self-mutilation like cutting. The patients' affect is unstable, showing marked reactive moods of irritability, anxiety, or mania, as well as dysphoria that can last a few hours or up to a few days. Dysphoria is another way of saying deep sadness, but these patients also show intense, inappropriate anger and have difficulty controlling it, along with stress-related paranoia and severe dissociative symptoms. When people disassociate, they feel disconnected from reality and from themselves, detached from their bodies and the world around them; sometimes, people don't even know they're doing it because this is the brain's way of coping with the stress that comes from enduring trauma. (Note: I have spent the past several years learning more about this personality disorder, and due to recent studies, there's some a suggestion that it will be removed from the DSM and integrated into the diagnosis of C–PTSD, complex post-traumatic stress disorder.)

3. Narcissistic personality disorder: This personality disorder goes a little deeper than just describing people who like to take tons of selfies and are completely enamored with themselves. Narcissism is viewed on a spectrum where healthy narcissism is very real, but so is malignant or unhealthy narcissism, which leads to abusive behaviors. These patients show a pattern of grandiosity with a need for admiration and a lack of empathy, the pattern beginning in early adulthood. You will see this quality in children because they are lacking the empathy that comes with a prefrontal cortex, making them little narcissists, but as they grow up, most children slowly begin to see that the

whole world doesn't revolve around them and that they'll have to consider others if they wish to have harmonious and healthy relationships with others. If the shell of narcissism isn't broken in childhood, then an adult emerges with an exaggerated sense of importance—a need to be recognized as superior—so they'll embellish their achievements. This type is preoccupied with fantasies of unlimited success, power, beauty, and/or ideal love. They believe that they are special and unique and should only associate with others of the same imagined caliber. There is an unrealistic sense of entitlement with expectations of favorable treatment, and they take advantage of others for personal gain, as well as often being arrogant and haughty, showing a lack of empathy for the needs of others. This personality disorder rarely shows up in therapy because they truly don't see anything wrong with their behavior and will blame others for the circumstances in their lives.

4. <u>Antisocial personality disorder</u>: These patients show a pattern of behavior starting around age 15 that demonstrates a lack of regard for the rights, safety, and volition of others. They are deceitful, as demonstrated by repeated lying, and they use aliases or con others for personal profit or pleasure. They refuse to conform to societal norms or laws and are repeatedly arrested, so they often end up with long rap sheets. They are reckless with the safety of others, impulsive, aggressive, and repeatedly engage in physical fights or assaults. Their consistent irresponsibility makes it impossible for them to hold down a job or be financially solvent. Finally, they lack remorse and instead justify their behaviors and rationalize why they hurt, steal, or mistreat others. (DSM-5, 2013)

The behaviors associated with Cluster B are what I've noticed to be pain points that bring people to therapy. In part, this is how I know that they are traits and not disorders—because people with disorders believe that their behavior is normal and are not looking for therapy.

Our last group in the personality disorders is Cluster C, the "withdrawn" group marked by intense feelings of anxiety and behaving in fearful ways. The personalities in this group are avoidant, dependent, and obsessive-compulsive.

1. <u>Avoidant personality disorder</u>: These patients show a pattern of social inhibition, feelings of inadequacy, and hypersensitivity to negative feedback.

They avoid occupational activities that involve interpersonal contact because of their extreme fear of criticism, rejection, and disapproval. They get involved with people only if they know they will be liked. In social settings, they are overly preoccupied with being criticized or rejected, viewing themselves as socially inept, personally unappealing, or inferior to others. Their fear of shame and ridicule prevents them from getting involved in relationships or participating in any new activities, as they want to avoid any sort of embarrassment.

2. Dependent personality disorder: These patients feel an excessive need to be taken care of, which leads to submissive and clingy behavior enacted to cope with their fear of separation. They relinquish control over their lives to others and have a difficult time expressing disagreement. Their lack of self-confidence causes impairment in starting projects or doing things, all due to a fear of judgment. They feel helpless when alone and go to great lengths to obtain nurturing and support from others. They are unrealistically preoccupied with the fear of being left alone and will, therefore, quickly seek out another relationship when one ends.
3. Obsessive-compulsive personality disorder: These patients show a pattern of preoccupation with orderliness, cleanliness, perfectionism, and mental and interpersonal control at the expense of flexibility or

> openness. They are preoccupied with details, rules, lists, order, schedules, and/or organization. They can be excessively devoted to work and their productivity, to the exclusion of any leisure activities. They are rigid around areas involving morals, ethics, or values, showing significant stubbornness in these areas. They have a hard time discarding objects, even when they have no sentimental value. They are also reluctant to delegate tasks because they don't feel that anyone else can do things in the way they expect them to be done. They are also miserly in spending, believing that money is something to be hoarded for future catastrophes. (DSM-5, 2013)

The classification of behaviors into disorders is helpful for understanding, identifying, and putting names to behaviors. As I continue to see people heal in treatment and begin thriving in their lives, I know that an individual can grow—changing their belief systems, values, and feelings as necessary, leading them to a vibrant personality and life. Using disorders to box someone in puts them in a defeated, complacent state; it may lead to patients believing that this is as good as it gets and that the poor behavior being pointed out is just part and parcel of who they are. If they believe that they are fundamentally broken, then they will not put forth any effort to try to improve themselves, even though such transformation would then improve their quality of life and relationships. In the end, we have to acknowledge that it's important to give people an opportunity to grow, but also recognize when they don't want to.

Cognitive Distortions

Having a personality disorder darkens your perception and view of the world, often taking it into a negative and dangerous place. When a person's thoughts and feelings are outside normal limits, we refer to them as *cognitive distortions*. It's these distortions that continue to keep a person mentally ill, as cognitive distortions are our mind's way of qualifying or disqualifying information based on what we believe, value, and feel. Letting go of these unhealthy thinking patterns means introducing and repeating new patterns that you are capable of creating—with help and persistence, of course. To become your authentic self, you'll need to peel away all of the layers of your false self that you've been assigned to make yourself fit in. Every time you create another false self, you buy into another narrative and create an identity and beliefs from that description. The problem that comes from abandoning the authentic self is an inner void, with a you that so desperately wants to live freely, but feels like it can't. Cognitive distortions hold the false parts of us in place, but learning new patterns allows our authentic self to emerge.

The factors considered in the psycho, spiritual, and social components also tell you who you're supposed to be and how you're supposed to behave. Your culture, for example, defines gender roles for you, and acceptable behaviors are defined within those roles, so if you attempt to stray from what's been defined for you, you'll then be rejected from your group. This is a problem since humans are tribal; we need people for that sense of belonging, which is why we're so readily able to give up our authentic selves for the sake of that belonging. This constant abandonment of our true self leads to those feelings of emptiness and despair that we've discussed. We crave being seen and being heard, and yet, who we really are and how we really feel is often buried deep under the version of ourselves that we know will be liked and accepted.

What must be noted is that being liked and approved of comes from the way we see ourselves through the eyes of those who mean the most to us. Those nods, smiles, and accolades that we receive help us know we mean something and are worth loving. Think about when you were younger and those messages you got—or the lack thereof. When those messages are absent or inconsistent, then our sense of self also becomes unstable. This instability causes us to feel unsure of ourselves and colors the way we perceive the world around us. It puts dysfunctional thinking into place. The most common cognitive distortions that we will look at are:

1. Labeling: Labeling is considered a distorted thinking style, as it positions you for defeat by defining who you are by your perceived flaws. For example, thinking "I'm fat" or "I'm stupid" is defining myself by those labels/insults, and thus it's because of those labels that a person can feel rejected, sad, and depressed. To choose one or more of your perceived flaws or characteristics and make a judgment based solely on them (because they're defining how you see yourself and thus defining your choices) boxes you in and prevents you from pursuing anything outside of that box—because labels *create* limitations. Labels are generally not used in positive ways, but rather to highlight inadequacies, so if you believe that you can't do x, y, or z because of your labels, then you likely won't even bother to try. And if you label yourself, you will also label others, as this helps you create control and support your own distortions. For example, saying "fat people are lazy" is a way of labeling others, and it limits your belief about them while also leading to hurt feelings and discord.

Self-Exploration Exercise:

Spend some time now writing down all the labels that you have assigned for yourself. What is the narrative that's being created because of those labels? Is it accurate? Is it limiting? How is it adding value to your sense of self? Next to each label, write down: A. If it's true and how you know that. B. Is it helpful to your growth? Why? Or why not? And C. What would be different if you no longer carried the label? Asking yourself these questions helps you to pay attention to the labels that you've assigned to yourself. If you removed them, what would you be able to achieve?

2. Personalization/blame: Personalization is blaming oneself or taking responsibility for things that were not your fault. Blame is another way to make sense of things—even if it's not true or fair. For example, if I'm a teenager, I might think, "My parents fight because I'm failing math, and because I'm stupid, they're getting divorced." It sounds completely ridiculous to read that out loud, but sadly, it's accurate to the thoughts of so many. Personalization causes a person to believe that everything others do or say is related to them and that everything is personal. This creates a feeling of inferiority and a constant need to compare oneself to others to once again qualify or disqualify one's worth.
3. Jumping to conclusions: Jumping to conclusions can be broken down into two specific behaviors—fortune-telling and mind-reading. Fortune-telling is when a person's thoughts create predictions based on

another person's behaviors, and mind-reading is imagining that we know what another person is thinking. There are some circumstances in which you will be right about what happens next because you've learned to identify patterns in people—especially since sometimes those closest to you will behave in very predictable manners, given how well you know them. But it's when you attempt to assign that template of thinking to others that it becomes problematic. Jumping to conclusions usually makes for negative conclusions based solely on a person's thoughts and intangible evidence. By forcing yourself to believe that a situation is the way you perceive it to be or predicted it to be, you're also predicting the outcome of how you'll feel. You'll feel sad, anxious, depressed, or angry based on the fabrications of your mind and not rooted in any truth other than your own, thus perpetuating your own misery. Mind-reading processes through that same faulty filter. For example, I might think, "I am fat and ugly, so there's no way they would want me" or "My ideas are stupid, so no one will ever listen to them." Notice how leaning toward the negativity gets in the way of attempting new things because of a lack of belief in oneself. In these mindsets, even if someone attempts to say or do something positive for you, you'll find a way to discount that as one cognitive distortion flows into another, and so if good things happen, then there's a reason for that, too—and it's also negative.

4. Disqualifying the positive: Disqualifying the positive is a distortion that throws away any good thing that happens to you or dismisses a person's positive behavior toward you. You'll tell yourself it doesn't count or that there was some motive behind it. For example, it might sound like this: "My boss/partner/friend only said this positive thing about me because they have to, or because they feel sorry for me." This disqualification happens because the idea of something good being equated with you is too foreign a concept for you to grasp. This makes having relationships challenging, in the sense that the other person will feel like they always have to prove that what they're saying to you is true—because you don't believe any positive thing they say. This demonstrates how and why inner worth can't simply be an outside job, as no amount of praise or validation will penetrate the tightly held negative beliefs that you have about yourself.

   Try to keep in mind here that no one owes you anything, so any time someone takes the time to share something positive about you, that is a gift. As uncomfortable as that may be to receive, take the gift and simply say "thank you" rather than telling the person 100 reasons why what they're saying isn't true. By not allowing yourself to receive such gifts from others, you're playing into your own confirmation bias of you being unworthy or not good enough to receive the praise or love that others want to give you.

Try using visualization to help you become more accepting of positive feedback or love. Imagine the other person is handing over a beautifully wrapped gift, and they took the time to emphasize all of the details, from wrapping paper to ribbons, because they want to celebrate you. Not allowing someone to celebrate you by not taking that gift from them is like you smacking the gift right out of their hands. This is also a good time to think about how you might feel if you took the time to pick out the perfect gift for someone, and when you handed it over, it was just knocked out of your hands. That's essentially what disqualifying the positive does to your relationships.

5. <u>All or nothing thinking</u>: All or nothing thinking, also referred to as "black or white thinking," creates a rigid stance on how things are supposed to look. Becoming more flexible in your thinking will require you to see the different shades of grey that life is and to stop viewing it as either black or white. This cognitive distortion is the breeding ground for perfectionism because its rules are that you either do something perfectly or you're a failure—and there's no room for anything in between. Individuals who engage in black and white thinking see things in extremes; things are either all good or all bad and without a middle ground. This means the mode of thought comes along with negative moods, feelings, and eventually depression. It's a predictable cycle that immediately

qualifies or disqualifies someone and leaves no room for growth. This is a fixed state for the person engaging in it and anyone that is in the person's life; couples do this, too, by engaging in "you always" or "you never" dialogue, which then boxes the other person into a fixed state and traps them there. Breaking this pattern will require you to start looking for the gray and avoiding those absolute terms like *nothing*, *never*, *always*, *can't*, etc. When things are black or white, they also come with rules for how a person should behave, what they can/can't do, or how they should have handled any given situation.

6. Should/must: *Shoulda, woulda, coulda* is another distortion that contributes to feeling like trash by means of guilt and shame. It's a state of judgment for not having made a better decision and leaves no room for trying again or (more importantly) for self-forgiveness. If you *shoulda* on yourself and judge your mistakes with a heavy hand, you'll likely do that to others, too—like when your partner or loved one does something differently from what you might have done, and you lean in with shaming them by saying things like, "You should have asked me, and then this wouldn't have happened."

   I've learned that people already feel really bad when they make poor choices, so *should*ing on them is essentially shitting on them. Instead, you have to try to leave room for choice and autonomy, and when mistakes happen, know that the ownership only falls on the person who made a mistake, even if the consequences extend to others. Try offering encouragement to yourself first and a commitment to try again with the knowledge gained from making the mistake in the first place. Experience is the most effective teacher, too, so leaving room for people to grow from their mistakes helps them to become the best version of themselves. Injecting *should* or *must* into your thought patterns perpetuates anxiety and stress, leading to procrastination. Allowing yourself to make choices and accepting failure does not have to shake your inner worth because knowing that you're not perfect allows you to accept perfectly imperfect you and allows you to try again.

7. Mental filtering: Mental filtering leads to anxiety and depression because the filter that is created to process thoughts is only connected to negative aspects of the situation and blocks out any positive ones. People on the journey to healing will often do this whenever an old feeling or behavior pops up. It forces them to go into the inadequacy and hopelessness loop and lose sight of all the hard work they've done up until that moment.
8. Magnification/minimization: Magnification and minimization distorted thinking is seen when people minimize how far they've come or the progress they have made. Instead of being able to see the big pic-

ture, they may hyper-focus on some perceived failure that destroys their entire effort. For example, you see it in the thought, "I was eating so healthy, and then I had a chocolate cake and blew my entire diet." This person may even have lost 20 pounds, but they're unable to see the progress because of the magnification perceived by the defined slip-up of eating chocolate cake. This form of distorted thinking seeks only to highlight your flaws while discounting any of your accomplishments. With this in mind, take some time here to think about ways that you do this to yourself. And remember that if you do this to yourself, you are likely doing it to others, too. In relationships, it's not uncommon for one person to feel like they aren't allowed to make mistakes—because when they do make a mistake, everything "good" that they've ever done no longer counts, allowing discouragement to set in with a feeling of them never being good enough. People are neither all good nor all bad, and we can continue having conversations about areas of opportunity while continuing to show appreciation for current and past efforts.

9. <u>Overgeneralizing</u>: Overgeneralizing judges a person's one single behavior and assigns a broad conclusion about them based on that single behavior. For example, someone says that they'll call you and then they don't, so you immediately decide that they're flaky and uninterested. This overgeneralization leaves no

room for that person's truth, as it assigns a pattern without gathering enough data to predict one. A child doing poorly on one math or music test may be told that it's because they are not musically or mathematically inclined, rather than that it was just one bad grade on one test. For that child, this could mean that instead of continuing to explore a skill or hobby, they'll talk themselves out of it and convince themselves to move in another direction because of the narrative that they lack or are not capable of success in an area where, realistically, they've barely begun exploring.

10. Emotional Reasoning: Emotional reasoning is a distortion that says, "Because I feel this way, it must be true." I often write in my captions that one's feelings are valid and deserve to be explored, but that we are never to assume that our feelings are facts. The danger in interpreting situations through our feelings comes from the changes to our mental states that are based on those thoughts—such as a person feeling anxious leading them to impulsivity or a person feeling anger leading them to lash out. By not allowing yourself an opportunity to stabilize and reach a neutral state, you invite consequences into your life. Allowing yourself a little time to settle down is helpful, and it's worth noting that the brain needs about 20 minutes to reframe a situation and allow you to respond appropriately.

If we are to continue to develop, grow, and mature emotionally, then we must start with reflecting on our thoughts. Seek to identify when you're falling into these faulty thinking patterns, if it doesn't feel right, it's not so ask yourself if there's another way to look at things. Allowing yourself to consider other ways of looking at things will not only help you to feel better emotionally, but will also improve your relationships with others. Becoming more flexible increases your emotional intelligence and your worldview because it allows you to see people for who they are and to hear them for what they're actually saying—not just what you're understanding. You'll need to increase your awareness around your thoughts and practice mindfulness to catch yourself and implement a new filter, but you can challenge your distortions in a number of different ways.

Challenging these cognitive distortions starts with admitting that they're there. Once you see that healing begins and ends with you, then you can choose to approach the challenge without resentment and hesitation (which would inevitably cause you to fail). Instead, you can embrace this opportunity to create a defining moment in your life and your mental state by taking control of it.

We want to accept ownership for mental wellness from here on out. Ownership is looking for all behaviors that reinforce the beliefs around why you are the way you are and why you want to change that narrative for the future.

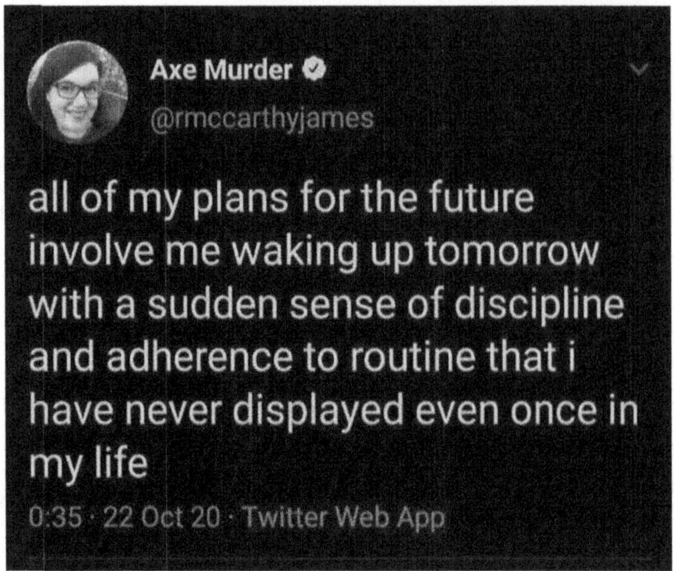

Self-Exploration Exercise:

Take the time now to write down on a piece of paper the self-limiting beliefs that you're carrying around. Look at the cognitive distortions above and think about the beliefs that they've led you to carry around. Create a table for yourself to use as a template to help get you started. Make three columns and label them accordingly as follows:

Column 1. Define the Self-Limiting Belief – [Example: I'm lazy.]

Column 2. What's the Behavior Being Reinforced? [Example: Over/under-exercising and giving up in 72 hours.]

Column 3. What's a Reframe Opportunity? What Small Habits Will Lead to Long-Term Change? [Example: It's a marathon, not a sprint, so I can start again tomorrow.]

Define the Self-Limiting Belief	What's the Behavior Being Reinforced?	What's a Reframe Opportunity? What Small Habits Will Lead to Long-Term Change?
[Example: I'm lazy.]	[Example: Over/under-exercising and giving up in 72 hours.]	[Example: It's a marathon, not a sprint, so I can start again tomorrow.]

The table is useful for asking yourself to search for all of the ways your limiting beliefs have caused you to stay stuck or only competent. The more distortions you discover and reframe, the more freedom you'll have.

With repetition of the reframes, you'll feel more optimistic and motivated to continue with your newly defined belief or behavior. While I realize that there's not a cure for everything, human beings can transform their lives in the most amazing ways and beat a diagnosis. I also know that a resilient human spirit who is committed to getting better will be consistent with their self-care, allowing for stability. We have new research emerging every day that demonstrates the power of thought quality on disease prognosis, as demonstrated in a powerful documentary called *HEAL*[7] that shows this theory in play. It examines the refusal of accepting a defeated status and how that will compel you to rise each day, seeking the better version of yourself. A better version of yourself comes from questioning yourself and asking yourself to find the supporting data for your thoughts. How do you know what you're thinking is true? Who told you that? Are they a reliable source? Why or why not?

When you're engaging in behavior that causes you to feel ill, sad, depressed, discouraged, or shamed, why should you accept that as your predestined state? Is it because you were taught that this is as good as it gets? Is that helpful to you or hurtful? Once you answer the questions, then you can ask yourself if there is another way to look at a self-limiting belief or, better yet, create a whole new narrative for your life that is complete with the values, attributes, and beliefs of a higher version of yourself. How would this higher version of you perceive the situation? How might they consider all the different aspects of it? To those of you in therapy, how would your therapist perceive this situation?

If life isn't working for you the way you had hoped, now what? I'll share with you that "Now what?" was one of those phrases that used to trigger an emotional reaction whenever my therapist used it. Sometimes that emotion was anger over her asking me, "Now what?" about circumstances that had happened to me that were not my fault. I wondered, how

7 HEAL Documentary 2017: Scientists and spiritual teachers discuss how thoughts, beliefs, and emotions impact human health and the ability to heal.

dare she suggest that I had to fix what someone else's negligence had created? After I stopped seeing red, though, I knew she was right, that the reasons I leaned toward depression and mental illness were because I hadn't created for myself an acceptable lens to view things through, to make necessary changes despite what had happened. Every time "Now what?" was posed, I was thrust into a state of cognitive dissonance. Cognitive dissonance occurs when there are contradictions in your thoughts, beliefs, or attitudes, and because of these contradictions, there are behavioral changes that need to be made. With my clients, I refer to this as the lifting of the veil; a veil clouds your vision, and when you remove it, you'll see something—and when you see something, you'll do something.

If the idea of a new narrative or accessing a higher version of yourself feels too overwhelming at first, try to reframe things by asking yourself what you might say to a good friend if they were sharing the same story with you. In other words, if your friend were thinking/feeling what you're experiencing, what would you say? Most people tend to be kinder and encouraging to others, forgetting to apply that same generosity to themselves. Another consideration is to solicit advice and feedback from friends or people you admire. If you don't have any who you trust to help you see things through a different lens, then hiring a professional would be useful, as outside help gives us tools to look inside of ourselves. Really, that's what all of this is about—looking inside of yourself to find the areas of life that are not working, seeking to understand why, and then finding ways to change the future outcomes. The way you feel about yourself and your capabilities also contributes to your success. You cannot fake any of this work because, when you try to fake it, those old patterns deeply defined in your brain will pick up where they left off, and the cycle will continue again.

You can build new pathways in your brain, though, and you must be consistent with those changes for them to stick. It's a constant and intentional checking in with yourself that will make the difference, as well as filtering through the new patterns that make them stay in place. And the longer you engage in these new patterns, the more they'll become your new normal, and the more you'll transform into the better version of yourself. After that, it's all the more likely that your future narrative will improve. With a new pathway to deal with old problems, you're giving your brain a choice to go left where it always gets hurt or to go right where it may feel uncomfortable, but results in a better outcome. Keep going right.

It's a lot of work. I hear that said by clients all the time, and I know it's true because I've been doing it myself for decades now. It's my own story that compels me to teach you more than anything else—because making sense of everything that I have endured has helped me to find a purpose in life, and that pushes this pen across the paper faster than anything I've ever read in a textbook. In fact, my education was a supplement to my healing, but I didn't know that at the time. As I learned theories and techniques, I also learned that things that happened to me had names, that they weren't okay, and that maybe I didn't have to be so incredibly hard on myself. Maybe, if I could learn to let go of my needs to control and manipulate for control, I could possibly have a better quality of life made possible through that very letting go.

Letting go turned into a defining moment in my life, as it leads to forgiveness, vulnerability, compassion, and true self-love. And while I agree that it is hard work, it's not the kind of hard work you dread doing every day. Instead, it's one that compels you to get up and try every day. I read somewhere that a therapist is only able to take a client as far as they have gone themselves, and when I read that, I thought to myself: *Challenge accepted.* That's the mindset you want to aim for.

I continue to be committed to leaving no stone unturned—to reflect, to engage in introspection, to ask the hard questions first of myself and then of you. If you can imagine a life worth living, then you're ready to begin building it. Healing is a messy process of coming completely undone, examining the broken pieces, and then reassembling them.

To prepare yourself for the healing section of this book, I'd like you to take a blank piece of paper and write your name in the center of it. Next, I want you to write down all of the things that you believe yourself to be and all of the things that "they" have told you that you are. Fill that page with as many things as you can think of, both good and bad, and when you've filled the page, I want you to start tearing off pieces one by one. Tear that sheet of paper up until there is nothing but a pile of paper with words in front of you.

Now, go grab some tape and put back the pieces you appreciate and that you find true; that new sheet of paper with its imperfect edges is the new you. It's okay if it doesn't look the way they said it was supposed to look, too—you get to define what it looks like next because you're in control now. You're capable of learning and doing hard things. The rebuilding process is done with one core objective in mind . . . *authenticity*. Create a more genuine and authentic version of yourself by fully accepting all of your flaws and loving yourself despite them.

> It's time to write a new story

Steps to Healing

Becoming the best version of yourself and building a life that you can be proud of involves a whole lot of healing. Healing has four parts:

1. Healing of your past traumas
2. Understanding emotional flashbacks and dissociation
3. Building of your self-worth
4. Identifying and removing the faulty filters and defense mechanisms that get in your way.

We build self-awareness in this process, and that contributes to your mental wellness by inviting you to truly know yourself. Knowing yourself builds inner trust and creates feelings of acceptance and inherent worth. It's knowing your strengths and weaknesses without triggering yourself into a shame response. Healing means taking responsibility for your thoughts and behaviors going forward, and it is an uncomfortable and often painful process involving a lot of time spent in introspection.

Introspection is defined as the examination or observation of one's own mental and emotional processes. For this to be done effectively, you must have an objective and a nonjudgmental stance when it comes to the review of your life and the traumas you've endured. This type of work is completely foreign for some of you, and seeking out a skilled helper who can teach you how to approach your past with curiosity and understanding is useful. Such a professional will also help you identify your emotional blind spots along the way, but with a nonjudgmental stance that blocks the lens of criticism and contempt (as that can only serve to make you feel worse than you already do). Developing a loving and trusting relationship with a better version of yourself means intentionally healing your past traumas while offering yourself sympathy and forgiveness for the parts of you that have caused you to feel ashamed, embarrassed, humiliated, rejected, or horrible in any way. The better version of you needs to be loved through it all and forgiven for everything you participated in, contributed to, or allowed to happen when you didn't know better. It's all so that you can now make a pact with yourself that, because you now know better, you will now do better, as well.

Processing what has happened to you and the decisions you've made along the way comes with questioning everything you've been taught and told. This has to happen for you to offer yourself the opportunity to determine what is useful and what's no longer aligned with who you are and who you are becoming. You will be able to identify patterns in how you make choices and in your behaviors, and then you'll learn techniques for how to rewire and reprogram the way you think and behave to be aligned with the most authentic version of yourself.

And, one last thing here: always remember that personal growth is a lifelong process and that we are to embrace it as something that we get to do for ourselves because of the love that we now have for ourselves.

Defense Mechanisms as Barriers to Mental Wellness

When trauma or anything painful occurs, our natural reflex is to drop out of the present moment and protect our mental health through the use of various (and often unhelpful) coping tools. Among them are defense mechanisms, which are unconscious mental processes used to avoid conscious conflict and the feelings of anxiety. The understanding of defense mechanisms was originally given to us by the father of psychology, Sigmund Freud—a psychoanalyst who stated that an individual's behavior is completely unconscious. Defense mechanisms are completely normal, and allowing yourself the time to learn which you're using and are keeping you from healing is helpful. We use defense mechanisms to keep faulty filters and negative belief systems in place. So, to rewire our thinking and behaviors, we'll need to understand what they are and how to recognize them and then offer ourselves a way to reframe them.

In these next few pages, we will look closely at ten commonly used defense mechanisms generally known as denial, repression, projection, displacement, regression, rationalization, sublimation, reaction formation, compartmentalization, and intellectualization. They may sound complicated, but with a basic understanding of them, you can catch yourself using them and ask yourself to choose another option. Becoming more aware of your defense mechanisms will help you to identify your faulty filters and beliefs by asking yourself questions as to why you would engage in that manner. Allowing yourself to become more curious about your behaviors and less judgmental will also allow you to think more flexibly. Processing your thoughts and behaviors this way will engage your rational mind and turn off your impulsive, emotional mind.

1. Denial: The most commonly used defense mechanism, denial, causes a person to refuse to accept facts or reality. This person will block out or deny memories that are not aligned with or in support of their beliefs about how something happened. Denial can be so strong that, if you know someone living in denial, you'll find yourself shaking your head in disbelief over how hard they work to keep that defense mechanism in place. Denial

can be useful in that it helps to protect us from having to experience the pain associated with something that's happened, but it often prevents us from taking very important steps to change current circumstances. Breaking up with denial must include ownership and accountability when it comes to the circumstances involved and taking responsibility for your part in whatever happened.

Substance abuse, as with alcoholism, is a classic demonstration of denial in action. While there are people capable of having a healthy relationship with alcohol, for others, it destroys their lives and the lives of those around them. People who abuse substances work hard at convincing themselves that they don't have a problem until the consequences of their actions become inescapable. According to the National Council on Alcoholism and Drug Dependence, alcohol is a factor in 40 percent of all violent crimes today, 37 percent of rapes and sexual assaults, 15 percent of robberies, and 27 percent of aggravated assaults (Staff, 2020). And the signs of a problem are pretty clear. If having drinks leads to black-out rages, you definitely have a problem. It's often from rock-bottom moments that the most amazing, defining moments emerge, though. Facing your fears and honestly evaluating the consequences of not addressing your problems is the only way to transform your life. When you face the emotions that you have been numbing yourself from and begin to validate your own experiences, you will begin to heal. It's time to stop pretending that what happened didn't or that it wasn't that big of a deal or that it doesn't matter if you're going to get better. All of the things that have happened to you need to matter to you, too.

2. Repression: Repression is our ability to send unwanted or painful thoughts deep into our unconscious, never to be heard from again. Like denial, repression is useful in keeping away unacceptable thoughts or desires, shutting them out of our conscious reality to prevent or minimize uncomfortable feelings that produce anxiety. Repression is commonly confused with suppression, which is consciously choosing to block out feelings or memories that cause uncomfortable feelings. The difference is that repression is an *unconscious* act. Briefly looking at phobias can help us understand repression a little better. For example, say a person is afraid of taking medication because they believe swallowing the pills may result in choking; they do not know why they're afraid of that happening—they just are. We learn that at age two, while being given cold medication, they choked on it, but because they have no recollection of the incident, they grow into an adult who has no memory of that episode and maintains a hypersensitive response or an extreme fear of swallowing (and choking on) medication. The fear that they experience is familiar, but because of their ability to repress painful memories, understanding it is not. The familiar feeling is also known as an emotional flashback. Traumatic experiences that happened to people without processing the experience afterward will often be repressed and then show up in how they

behave. This phenomenon can also be seen in victims of childhood sexual abuse, whose experiences remain hidden in their unconscious, but continue to interfere with their ability to sustain healthy romantic sexual relationships later in life. While repression of the memories protects the person's mental health, it then harms them in another way. Healing comes with identifying these lost parts/experiences/stories, hearing the story and validating it, and finally integrating the lost parts with the present self.

3. Projection: Projection comes when we assign uncomfortable feelings that we're holding onto to someone else rather than identifying the feelings within ourselves and dealing with them. This also happens with inappropriate behaviors when a person accuses someone else of something to avoid seeing it in their own behavior. An example of this is an arguing couple making accusations based on their own experiences. One will begin yelling and then accuse the other of always being so angry. Or in another case, a spouse who is cheating will constantly accuse the other of being unfaithful. When you tell someone how they feel, you are likely projecting your own feelings onto them, but because your own feelings are so uncomfortable, you are unable to connect to them. Active listening can help you to minimize projection because it involves asking yourself to paraphrase what you're hearing another person say in order to connect with how they're actually feeling and not how you *think* they're feeling. When having conversations, practice saying things like, "If I

understand you correctly, you are saying x." This allows the other person to then say, "Yes, that's exactly what I'm saying," or "No, what I'm saying is y." Practicing active listening will help you to improve your relationships with others and also manage your unconscious defenses.

4. Displacement: A great use of suppressed emotions, displacement is described by Freud as a person unconsciously transferring emotions from where they belong to an easier target. When we spend our lives pushing a negative emotion down, a slight trigger can create explosive reactions—such as road rage, for example. While it is extremely annoying to be cut off in traffic, to then follow someone home and beat them up would be excessive. But it might make sense if the person carrying out that behavior is also having an emotional flashback filled with rage due to another incident, whereby they feel powerless and unable to express themselves. When your behaviors and emotions are inappropriate to the present moment, displacement may be the cause, so learning how to stay grounded and present will help you to sort through your feelings and identify what belongs in the here and now versus what doesn't.

5. Regression: Whenever we are faced with uncomfortable and distressing emotions, we seek to escape from the pain that creates anxiety and revert to old behaviors even if they're dysfunctional—because they're comforting. This is regression. I have seen extreme cases of regression on those reality TV shows where people dress up like babies and have their partners take care of them. Regressing into

a childlike state is comforting, even if it's completely inappropriate, so learning self-soothing skills that are appropriate for the adult version of you can help you prevent yourself from regressing into a childlike state. Another example of this is temper tantrums; when intense anger has no healthy outlet, people will break things and yell or scream to express their feelings because they don't have the adult words to access—at the moment or at all. Paying closer attention to what you choose to do when you're in the moment of such stress is how you'll be able to ask yourself if the behavior you're choosing is aligned with the adult version of yourself that you now know you can be. And, if not, what could you be doing differently is the question to ask yourself next.

6. Rationalization: This defense is known as "making excuses" for either your own behavior or someone else's. When we use this defense mechanism, it helps us to try to make sense of things that just don't make sense. The goal here is to appease our minds and help us to slip back under the veil of consciousness and into another state of denial by hiding the truth. Rationalizations can be used in all types of scenarios to explain or justify abuse. Adult children raised by emotionally or physically violent caretakers will often rationalize their abuser's behavior as happening because the caretakers were stressed or say they were abused, and thus, they naturally became abusers, too. People in abusive relationships will rationalize the abuse as happening because their partner had a difficult

childhood, and they can't help themselves. But for you to heal, you must be willing to stop making excuses for poor behavior, or you will remain under the veil of consciousness, sleeping on yourself and your own interests. While it may be true that your partner, your friend, your parent, your caretaker, or whoever else hurt you had a difficult upbringing and terrible things happened to them, those terrible things happening to them do not justify them then abusing you. Two wrongs will never make a right, so do not allow yourself to make excuses for bad behavior.

7. Sublimation: As described by Freud, sublimation is a mature defense mechanism by which a person has transformed socially unacceptable impulses into socially acceptable behaviors. Being able to express intense emotions through positive means helps a person to release the impulse without harming themselves or others. Take anger, for example: Being able to redefine it and express it through a sport like boxing is a helpful release of it, while anxiety can be worked through by running, and sadness can be transformed through artwork. All of these are examples of taking negative emotions and transforming them into healthy expressions.
8. Reaction formation: This is an attempt to squash deep feelings of fear, shame, or anxiety to the point where a person will then develop the opposite belief in order to bury their own. Take, for example, a person ashamed of their homosexuality then becoming incredibly homophobic in an effort to hide their truth. Here, the reaction to

the stimulus is always big to hide the unconscious fears of one's desires rising to the surface. Another example of this is seen in hostage or kidnap victims who end up siding with the person who abducted them and caring for them, a condition known as Stockholm Syndrome.

9. Compartmentalization: This is the ability to keep difficult parts of one's life or experiences completely separate from others in order to avoid feelings of distress. It's easily seen in the first responder community, as oftentimes, our firefighters, police officers, and EMTs have to bear witness to gruesome crime at accident scenes, which then creates dissonance and distress. To maintain their mental health, they compartmentalize what they've seen as a way of protecting their psyche from the horrors they witnessed, so they can go home and participate in life with their families like nothing ever happened. Compartmentalization becomes harmful when a person seeks refuge by numbing themselves with substances, whether to block intrusive thoughts or to ease anxiety. A compartmentalized life allows for different parts to show up when necessary and others to be temporarily muted. A modern-day example is any meme that refers to your ability to turn off your "customer service" voice when you come home from work. This ability to have a work version of you, a home version of you, or whatever version of you that you need to create for a given circumstance is a demonstration of compartmentalization.
10. Intellectualization: This means that, by sticking to the

facts, one removes all of the emotions from a situation, so it's a sometimes cold and clinical defense strategy. By focusing on the facts of something, one doesn't have to connect with the painful feelings that are associated with that thing, such as being dealt a terminal diagnosis. The person dealing with that diagnosis may choose to educate themselves about it, though, to the exclusion of experiencing the crushing fear that comes with receiving it. Intellectualization causes a person to avoid experiencing painful feelings in the here and now. However, the thing to note about healing is that until we fully tap into our feelings and examine them, we don't heal. Gaining power and control over your life involves a deeper dive to uncover your defenses. Through this increased self-awareness, we're able to see patterns in our behaviors and remember that our behaviors are separate from who we are—and, therefore, they can be modified any time we choose.

Growing into a better version of yourself includes growing up emotionally and being willing to recognize the unhealthy and sometimes toxic thought patterns that result in making poor decisions. When you can identify the patterns, you can change them. Understanding your defense mechanisms will help you keep from reacting to your circumstances and help you to start responding in a way that allows you to be more vulnerable and authentic. As you grow, the things that were once acceptable to you may no longer be acceptable, and that's okay—it's okay for you to redefine yourself, and in fact, it's sometimes necessary.

Part 3: Trauma and Romantic Drama

"How are you single?"
Lmao you about to find out just hang tight buddy

Romantic relationships are often challenging for those who've endured abusive or dysfunctional childhoods. Unconsciously, these types choose partners that mirror the behaviors and characteristics of the caretaker relationships that were modeled to them. The absence of modeling is also found in single-parent homes or otherwise non-traditional settings like those of divorcees and widowers who choose not to date again, and the absence of a healthy romantic relationship seen via caretakers will also leave its prints on children. Toxic patterns are repeated in adult relationships as an attempt to unconsciously repair broken childhood relationships, and it's mostly in the context of romantic relationships that you are going to be triggered into the most insecure version of yourself. If you look, you'll be able to see how the love that you got or didn't get shows up in the relationships you have today. One glance at today's trending memes on social media will highlight the challenges of dating, the rate of toxic relationships, and our "scarcity mindset," suggesting there are only so many partners available to us. When there's a fear that there are no good people left out there for them to find, many will cling to unhealthy partners—believing anyone is better than no one.

Let's explore one of the reasons why you may cling to unhealthy relationships outside of the scarcity mindset theory. Take a moment to think about all of the relationships that you've been exposed to in your life, the most important being between your parents or primary caretakers. It can be hard to look at your parents or primary caretakers through any negative lens without feeling ashamed or ungrateful, but this exercise is not intended to take any of your love away or to create villains out of them; it truly is intended to help you begin thinking critically and peeling back the layers that will lead to you understanding yourself better. How they did things matters, and the less time we spend in denial of that, the more time we can spend feeling emotionally healthy and ready to engage in meaningful relationships. The relationships that your primary caretakers had with each other were modeled to you throughout your childhood, so understanding the impact that they've had on you and the way you show up in relationships today is critical to your growth. Becoming the best version of yourself will always be your responsibility, and learning to identify unhealthy patterns that were taught to you will help you to choose better partners.

If things are not working well for you romantically or you find yourself repeating toxic patterns, then learning is the only way for you to break those faulty, unconscious patterns that were taught to you. Based on my experience, instead of seeing the dysfunction in the relationship, people who do not have self-worth will instead blame themselves and believe that they are fundamentally broken and unlovable. They describe themselves as having a "clingy personality" or suggest their behavior is a trait assigned to them by their zodiac sign. But none of that will be helpful if you're trying to be a better version of yourself and enjoy healthy, fulfilling relationships. Whenever you are externalizing your power and control over your behavior, then you are accepting that this is as good as it gets for you—and that could not be further from the truth. No matter how old you are, growth will always require that you remain flexible with your thinking, as there will always be room for learning new patterns and emotional maturity.

Attachment Styles and Love

Biology teaches us that humans are designed for pair bonding. We are pulled toward each other first for mating and then for a variety of other reasons, including having someone to take on an all-inclusive trip to Mexico. We come together today looking for security, reliability, safety, emotional support, financial support, and a forever partner. The health and success of our romantic relationships, though, rely heavily on how romantic attachment is created. Let us spend some time learning about attachment and where it all began, in our childhoods.

John Bowlby was a British psychoanalyst, psychologist, and psychiatrist, and his attachment theories are among the most important contributions to the understanding of human connections. Having a working understanding of these attachment theories will give you a tremendous amount of insight into your own behavior. Once you can identify those patterns of behavior that are getting in the way of your ability to have healthy relationships, you will be able to learn how to modify those behaviors and replace them with healthier choices. It is empowering to know that you can change your behavior at any given point; once you recognize the patterns, you get to decide what happens next.

Bowlby's work showed that a child initially forms one primary attachment. This attachment is the foundation of security that tells the child to explore the world, and this then becomes the prototype for all future social relationships. Attachments are formed in four distinct ways and include the following characteristics:

1. Safe Place: The primary caretaker consistently provided comfort in times of distress, fear, or danger.
2. A Secure Base: The primary caretaker was reliable

and allowed the child to ask questions to help them continue learning and sorting things out.

3. Proximity Maintenance: The child felt safe to explore the world, knowing that they could return to the primary caretaker and receive nonjudgmental love and support.
4. Separation Distress: This is the degree to which a child becomes distressed when the primary caretaker leaves.

Alongside gaining an understanding of how attachments are formed, understanding your own attachment style will help you to make sense of your behaviors; you can reflect on your current and past relationships and see the patterns. While seeing those patterns may feel discouraging or overwhelming, keep in mind that you did not choose this for yourself. Also, this is not a fixed state, and you can choose new behaviors by learning to have patience and consistency with yourself. Being able to recognize others' attachment styles will also help you choose secure partners who'll then provide you safety within the relationship so that you can continue your growth and development together. Those four styles are:

1. Secure Attachment: When children have a healthy, secure attachment to the primary caretaker, they see themselves in a positive light. They feel valued, respected, and worthy. They show higher levels of emotional intelligence and can engage with others in meaningful ways. They're secure and confident in themselves because of the attachment they have

developed with their primary caretaker. In a secure attachment, the behavior of the primary caretaker is sensitive, consistent, supportive, and reliable. As a result, children will grow into healthy adults with boundaries. They can take ownership and accountability for their behaviors, and they will recognize others as separate individuals with their own valid emotions. They also remain flexible with their thinking and are always seeking ways to improve themselves and to understand others, making them a great romantic choice.

2. Anxious or Ambivalent Attachment: Children with this type of attachment style may cling to their primary caretaker and feel afraid to explore their environments on their own. If the primary caretaker leaves the environment, the child becomes inconsolable and has a hard time interacting—often choosing not to interact at all because of the distress involved. When they do engage, they demonstrate aggressive tendencies and have problems with regulating and controlling their negative emotions. The profile of the primary caretaker in this attachment style shows that they were inconsistent with their care of the child, showed indifference toward the child, and/or had an inner belief that they were incapable of providing for the child's needs. This child will develop trust issues and have abandonment fears. They will grow into adults who struggle with trust issues, abandonment,

and low self-worth. In relationships, they'll become overly dependent on their partners for comfort and security, and can be highly emotional and jealous, with low impulse control and unpredictable moods.

3. Avoidant Attachment: Children with an avoidant attachment often feel rejected by their primary caretaker and suffer from deep emotional isolation, often being stressed and scared. This child will actively seek to avoid their primary caretaker, likely because they are being physically or emotionally abused or neglected. The profile of this primary caretaker is one that rejects outward displays of emotion and refuses to acknowledge the child's cries, actively suppressing any display of emotion by telling them to shut up or to stop crying. When a child's emotions are shamed, they will then grow into adults who are emotionally unavailable, struggling with communication centered around emotions and avoiding commitment altogether. Consistently feeling rejected by their primary caretaker will then create a fear of rejection in all relationships, but especially in romantic ones. Not being able to trust anyone to provide love will cause them to get scared if anyone gets close enough to try. When someone attempts to get close to another with this attachment style, they may lash out and behave in aggressive ways, unconsciously triggering the abandonment that they feared all along and making them unhealthy romantic choices if they're not willing to work on themselves.

4. Disorganized Attachment: A child with a disorganized attachment style is often confused because there is no consistent pattern coming from their primary caretaker. These children often feel overly familiar with strangers and even seek safety from them. They have feelings of low self-worth, fear, sadness, and anger. The profile of the primary caretaker's behavior is marked by unpredictability. These primary caretakers are more likely to be addicts or have untreated mental illnesses, making it impossible for them to provide stability for the child. These children do not trust their primary caretakers and may lash out with aggressive behavior such as hitting and kicking; they also do very poorly in settings with other children. These children will grow into adults who struggle with managing their impulses and have difficulty soothing themselves in healthy ways, making them more susceptible to addiction and mental illnesses. In romantic relationships, they have a hard time opening up and are also emotionally unavailable. When a struggle for power and control comes up, they are more likely to lean toward abusive and toxic behaviors, making them another unhealthy romantic choice if they refuse to participate and grow as a person.

Your understanding of love on both a conscious and sunconscious level is created by the relationships that were modeled to you and your individual relationship with your primary caretakers. Your ability to love yourself and to love others also comes from the emotion you received or did not receive from those primary caretakers. When you don't love yourself or even hate yourself, it is important to ask where your lack of self-love came from so that you can explore it more closely instead of accepting it as your absolute truth. Think about the messages that were directly or indirectly sent to you by your primary caretakers. What did their metacommunication tell you about how they felt about you? Remember that metacommunication is everything that we say without opening our mouths. Do you remember the eye contact, the facial expressions, the body language? If you experienced anything other than a secure, loving attachment in your childhood, then you are more likely to be filled with negative inner sentiment toward yourself. Dismissive or abusive primary caretakers contribute to the emotional, spiritual, cognitive, and relational impairment of their children. Without any healthy influences, a child begins to blame themselves, which creates an inner critic with a relentless loop of messages that include worthlessness and feelings of hopelessness.

Intimate Partner Violence and Toxic Relationships

When you have a lower level of self-worth, you will then have a higher tolerance for toxic and dysfunctional partners. This happens when your primary caretakers modeled abuse, and you learned to function in dysfunction. Since abuse has been made to look and feel normal, anything healthy will then feel abnormal. According to the American Psychological Association, a child's exposure to a father abusing a mother is the strongest risk factor for transmitting violent behavior from one generation to the next.[8] Additionally, the Director of the Minnesota Center Against Violence and Abuse said that children who've experienced domestic violence are two to three times more likely to repeat the cycle of violence in adulthood compared to either the victim or perpetrator.[9] A little girl who watches her dad beat her mom learns that this is how conflict is managed, and even if she tries to protest their fighting, she realizes that she cannot stop it—and in order to stay safe, she must also stay quiet. She will then grow up and choose partners similar to her caretakers, who exhibit more aggressive and violent behavior. Then, when domestic violence shows up in her relationship, she will believe that it's the norm since it was taught to her through modeling. She is "malignantly optimistic" that things will get better. Malignant optimism was defined by Dr. Sam Vaknin as "the dysfunctional antithesis of a

8 Hamby, S., Finkelhor, D., & Turner, H. (2014, April 7).Intervention Following Family Violence: Best Practices and Helpseeking Obstacles in a Nationally Representative Sample of Families With Children. ***Psychology of Violence***. Published online. http://dx.doi.org/10.1037/a0036224

9 Bragg, H. Lien. ***Child Protection in Families Experiencing Domestic Violence***. US Department of Health and Human Services, 2003.

useful coping mechanism known as defensive pessimism. People refuse to believe that some questions are unsolvable, some diseases are incurable, some disasters inevitable. They see a sign of hope in every fluctuation. They read meaning and patterns into every random occurrence, utterance, or slip. They are deceived by their own pressing need to believe in the ultimate victory of good over evil, health over sickness, order over disorder. Life appears otherwise so meaningless, so unjust and so arbitrary, so they impose upon it a design, progress, aims and paths, this is magical thinking.

Violent families encourage secrecy and create justifications for abuse. They look to blame each other instead of taking ownership and accountability for their behaviors. This is dangerous because it creates a belief that the victim could somehow have stopped the abuse if they'd chosen to. For example, they might think, "If Mom would have just kept her mouth shut, Dad would not have had to hit her." When a child is exposed to a primary caretaker who is sometimes good and sometimes bad, they will then lean toward partners who have the same characteristics to create their own version of normal. The unconscious coding that is being written here is that love equals violence. There are several other factors that also contribute to intimate partner violence; however, in this book, we are focused on early childhood conditioning and its impact on romantic relationships. And while this may seem like an extreme generalization, the statistics on intimate partner violence are alarming.

According to the Centers for Disease Control (CDC),

one in four women and one in seven men will experience physical violence at the hands of their intimate partners. Our national statistics show that an average of nearly 20 people per minute are physically abused. (Control, Center for Disease Control, 2018) Let us take a closer look at the three most common types of intimate partner violence, formally referred to as domestic violence. The CDC breaks down intimate partner violence into four types of behavior.

1. Physical Violence: This is defined as a person hurting or trying to hurt a partner by hitting, kicking, or using any other form of physical force.
2. Sexual Violence: This is defined as forcing or attempting to force a partner to take part in a sexual act, sexual touching, or a non-physical sexual event such as sexting, sending nudes, or watching porn. Being in a committed relationship never gives you free access to your partner's body; consent must always be given.
3. Psychological Aggression: This is the use of verbal and non-verbal communication with the intent to harm another person mentally or emotionally and/or to exert control over another person.
4. Stalking: This is a pattern of repeated, unwanted attention and contact by a partner that causes fear or concern for one's own safety or for the safety of someone close to the victim. (Control, Center for Disease Control, 2018)

Intimate partner violence knows no gender boundaries and is not solely related to the typical stereotype of men being the aggressors against women, as we now know from the courageous men coming forward to share their stories. We now also know that over 43 million women and 38 million men have experienced psychological aggression from an intimate partner in their lifetimes. (Control, Center for Disease Control, 2018) I have seen that shame is one of the main reasons that so many people stay silent. Shame then leads to blame, as well, with victims blaming themselves for being treated poorly, feeling shame for putting themselves in a given situation without giving enough thought to the programming they received that contributed to them blindly entering into the relationship and then repeating the patterns.

When all you've known is red flags, they'll be hard to identify. To begin building a healthy understanding of love, start with asking yourself what you believe love is. How does your understanding translate into behaviors? Looking at your current understanding of love will help you to see your faulty patterns and replace them.

What Is Love and What Is Healthy?

My girlfriend be like "I know a place" then take me to the happiest most healthy point in my life

Self-Exploration Exercise:

If, after reading through all of this, you feel confused

about what love is because of what was taught to you when you were a child, let's do some exploring about your understanding of love.

The exploring love exercise was developed by a spartan life coach, Richard Grannon.[10] For this exercise, you will take a blank sheet of paper and draw three vertical lines for three columns, all on one page. Grannon recommended that you allow yourself an hour of uninterrupted time to explore this exercise, to discover all of your unconscious beliefs around love. In column number one, you will list all of the things that you love about love.

Column 1: What I love about love:

Not being alone

Having someone to do things with

When you are done listing, write out why this is desirable to you right next to each of those items.

In the second column, list all of your current and past beliefs about love.

Column 2: Love is:

Violent

Transactional

Performance-based

Sacrificial

Keeping score

Once you have created your list, reflect on the attachment style that makes the most sense to you and then make

10 I spoke to Richard Grannon in the summer of 2019 to discuss his work. He offers tremendously useful mental health content on his YouTube channels, so check him out!

correlations between what you believe love to be and the behavior that was modeled to you by your primary caretakers. Challenge yourself to complete this exercise often so that you can continue to build on your understanding, asking yourself to be honest about what you have learned based on what you've seen and what you're currently doing in your relationships.

In the third column, you'll list what you believe to be ideal or healthy about love (even if you are not currently practicing it). It's important for you to create new connections in your brain surrounding healthy love, and with enough repetition, you will begin to believe and lean toward healthier behaviors.

Column 3: Healthy Love is:

Respectful

Kind

Boundaried

Reciprocal

Supportive

Here's an example of what the table looks like:

What do I love about love?	What are my current/past beliefs about love?	What do I now believe healthy love should look like?
Doing things together	Love is a transaction	Mutual respect

Creating Boundaries and a Sense of Self

If we're dating, I want to be your second priority.

I want your first priority to be you, your ambitions, your life and your future, because my priority right now, is me and mine.

Finding happiness and security alone, is crucial to finding it together.

As you reflect on the results of your self-exploration exercise, you'll discover the unhealthy beliefs around love that are causing you to repeat similar patterns in different relationships. When you've identified the ideal healthy qualities of love, you can reprogram the way you think about how love should look. By challenging yourself to think about love in ideal ways, you will also be improving your internal boundaries that are stored on an unconscious level. Remember that what happened to you as a child was never your fault, and that it is hard to do better when you do not know better. I want you to feel empowered by the knowledge that you will gain through this type of introspective exercise. When you can see what you are doing and understand why you are doing it, you can then begin working on the behaviors that are aligned with the person who you want to be. Becoming a better version of yourself begins with creating a new narrative around your understanding of love and what your expectations for it will be going forward. This may also show you changes that need to be made in your existing relationship. If you want a happier love story, you must create it.

Evolving into a better version of yourself will require you to forgive yourself for the choices you made when you didn't know any better. So many of you carry a giant heart that understands pain, and since you understand how pain feels, you are more likely to run toward the pain in others so that you can try to help them. You want to be able to help, and being needed also gives you a sense of purpose, but that right there is the setup for an unhealthy relationship. Before you can be healthy, you'll need to do some healing—because, without forgiveness toward yourself, you will not believe that you are deserving of better relationships. And that belief, combined with low self-worth, will cause you to allow more hurt into your life. Take the time to define love for the highest version of yourself who you can both admire and respect. That version will be able to establish standards and create boundaries to protect them. That version knows what they value, what's important, and most importantly, that version loves you so very much—all of you.

Healing will also help you to create boundaries that will aid you in staying in your own lane in relationships, as you want to be able to maintain a healthy give-and-take that promotes and encourages you both to demonstrate mutual respect. Giving yourself permission to create boundaries for the type of relationship that you would like to have will protect you from getting into more toxic relationships. Creating boundaries may feel overwhelming at first, especially if all you've been exposed to is dysfunctional. In that case, you may feel that you don't have the courage to enforce the boundaries that you are creating, but by the time you are done here, courage will be something that you'll have an abundance of. This is your opportunity to define yourself based on your own values and not those that were imposed upon you. Take the values that are useful for you and use them to build on, and then begin making decisions about the values that make sense for who you are and for the highest version of yourself that you are creating.

Self-Exploration Exercise:

To begin defining boundaries, you start by choosing your values. Make a list, asking yourself: *What is most important to you? Why is it important to you?* Your values will then translate into standards of behavior. Write those down, too. When you define what is important to you and how it's demonstrated, you will know what to create your boundaries around.

Spending this time defining boundaries for yourself will help you feel more confident about enforcing them with others. As you continue your growth and development, your values will also change so that you'll be able to continue building this value system for yourself as you go.

If you were never taught about boundaries, you should know that boundaries are the lines that you draw that teach people how to treat you. Boundaries help you say no when something does not work for you, but without feeling guilty or bad about it. That is what makes saying "no" so hard for so many of you—those feelings of guilt and shame that we are programmed into feeling any time we chose our own needs over someone else's. Take a moment to review your current belief system about what it means to choose yourself over others, as being able to choose yourself greatly contributes to your long-term success. If there are negative beliefs—such as saying "no" is selfish—then you will need to work on reprogramming those misbeliefs first, as those faulty beliefs will continue to get in the way of your growth. The saying goes that you cannot pour from an empty cup, and so it goes that being able to take care of yourself first will allow you to give the best version of yourself to others.

For your boundaries to stick, you will also need to have respect for yourself. Self-respect can be a challenge if you are carrying around a lot of shame. Shame suffocates your boundaries when it hasn't been fully processed. Shame is also a great source of fuel for your inner critic, as it'll say things like, "Who do you think you are, asking for respect? You did not respect yourself when you did (fill in the blank)!" Combatting shame is another argument for the benefits of forgiving the perfectly imperfect you. Boundaries only work when you see value in yourself. What happens if you do not see the value in yourself or take the time to establish healthy boundaries? In relationships without boundaries, you will feel exhausted because you are giving away more than you are receiving and allowing others to take advantage of you. When you allow others to take advantage of you, you will end up with feelings of resentment toward them for thinking that they should treat you the way that you treat them, and that is simply not true. No one is like you, so look for reciprocity before over-giving again. I once heard Richard Grannon say in one of his many incredibly useful YouTube videos that you are to stop allowing others to use you as an emotional dildo. That hit me like a dildo on the forehead. As a result, I began to associate a giant dildo with the people in my life that needed to go: the people that talked at me and not with me, the men that didn't care about my favorite food (which is pizza) or what my dreams were, the ones that would take my valuable time and use it to play with themselves. If I was going to achieve the goals I have for my life, this needed to stop. The first step was acknowledging what I had allowed. The next step was having the courage to ask for what I needed and then knowing when to go when my needs weren't met, or a compromise wasn't considered. I had to stop letting people use me as an emotional dildo, and so do you.

Thinking that others think the way that you do can also

cause you to be too trusting. And when you're too trusting, you'll miss the red flags in others because you're believing in the best version of them and completely missing the truth of who they are in the here and now. Simply put, a lack of boundaries prevents you from being able to hold others accountable for how they treat you and welcomes other dysfunctional relationship patterns such as codependency. Codependency is apparent in a relationship when one person relies on the other for all of their needs being met; their entire identity comes from who they are in the relationship, and they lack a sense of self outside of it. If this describes you, though, your current relationship did not make you codependent. Your codependency comes from having been raised in a dysfunctional family and/or having an addicted or mentally ill parent or caretaker. Since codependency programming begins in childhood, it will be hard to know that you are engaging in the behavior because it's your normal operating system, so let us take a look at some signs of codependency.

You might be codependent if:

1. You have a hard time saying no.
2. You often feel guilty for saying no.
3. You have feelings of low self-worth.
4. You need constant validation and/or are clingy.
5. You need to be needed or need someone to take care of.
6. You are rigid and have a need for control.
7. You have a hard time communicating your emotions.
8. You're afraid of rejection or abandonment.
9. You obsess and replay situations in your mind,

over-thinking yourself into an anxious state.

10. You're overly sensitive and/or highly reactive.

To break up with codependency, you will first be required to break up with denial. Denial that anything is wrong is what keeps you stuck in this place. Denial is itself kept in place with low self-worth and low self-esteem. When you start to see that this all developed because your feelings were invalidated and ignored when you were a child, then that might elicit a little self-sympathy for you and your experience. I have never met anyone who wanted to be pitied, and because pity is often associated with sympathy, it's something that people have a hard time offering themselves or allowing themselves to receive. Yet, having a little sympathy for yourself will encourage you to move in a growth direction because you'll realize that you've never had a choice in the matter. And now that you're able to offer that gift to yourself, you can start fresh and clean the slate. Being less codependent means becoming more independent, and that also means learning to do things for yourself and getting to know yourself better—which all lead to building a life that is aligned with who you're meant to be. This is an invitation to learn more about yourself. What are your interests? Your hobbies? Your passions? You have autonomy to make choices from an authentic place and not a forced-upon-you understanding of how things are supposed to look.

Self-Exploration Exercise:

Let's look at all the areas of your life that have been neglected because you've been so busy taking care of everyone else. Take a sheet of paper and write down the following headings: health, education, friendships, career, spirituality, hobbies, and other interests and relationships. Under each heading, list the ways that you currently participate in the category of your life, and then make another list of how you'd like to participate going forward. If you're seeing gaps or areas that need some help, set some goals for yourself in those areas and make a commitment to yourself that you will meet them. Then, create the boundaries that you'll need to put in place to protect your time so that you can achieve your goals. Your time is so incredibly valuable, and when you have goals worth pursuing, it's important to manage time properly, keeping your sights on what you need in order to achieve the bigger picture—which is ultimately an ability to say no to others and yes to yourself.

Example:

Education

1. Complete my degree.

Boundaries Needed:

Ask for help at home to carve out two hours to spend on schoolwork per week.

As you work on the creation of those goals and the management of your time, you may feel guilty about the work that you're doing, but it's important that you understand that guilt has been used as a way to control you. Remind yourself that you are allowed to focus on yourself and build a relationship with yourself without it being selfish. Sit with your uncomfortable feelings and remember that being denied the experience of your feelings is what got you here to begin with; be patient with yourself and allow yourself to feel. When you are used to being responsible for everyone else's feelings, you end up being extremely dismissive of your own feelings, so being able to identify and name them might be unfamiliar in the beginning.

It is important that you take as much time as you need to build a solid relationship with yourself. It's when you truly know who you are, what you like, and what you need that you'll be better able to identify what you don't like and what you don't need from others. This process may take you years, especially if you were raised in an environment that didn't celebrate your individuality or encourage autonomy, but that's okay. Building a healthy human who can relate to others in healthy ways will require patience and hard work, but it's the kind of hard work that makes you feel good instead of the hard work that has you repeating dysfunctional patterns and thus creating a heavy, depressing, and anxiety-ridden state of being. It's when you truly know yourself that you will be able to see the value and worth that's within you, and then, when you come to the table in a relationship, you'll hold yourself in higher regard and will choose partners who complement your life and encourage you to live authentically. Whenever the focus is on saving someone or being saved by someone, dysfunction will be invited in, leading you to abandon yourself again. That means you have to stay committed to building your identity, stay grounded, and remember that you can only control yourself.

Dating and Creating Standards

Once you're ready, you'll start dating and putting yourself out there, which is going to test the strength of the value system you've defined and the boundaries you've created for yourself. It is important that you remain humble in this process, never being too confident, because the pathways that lead to dysfunction are deeply embedded in your brain—and breaking up with them for good will require patience and consistency. Enforcing boundaries and asserting yourself will bring out all sorts of uncomfortable feelings, and uncomfortable feelings trigger us and may cause a regression in your newfound healthy behaviors. Don't be discouraged when you experience a step back, though; it doesn't mean that you're not capable of the change. It just means that you need to expect your old ways to try to creep back in during times when you are feeling vulnerable. If you can learn to expect this to happen, you'll be less likely to react to it by beating yourself up. Beating yourself up stops the entire glow-up process; everything must stop while you're entertaining thoughts of how awful and pathetic you are or what a loser or a whore you are, and there's just no time for that. On the road to becoming the best version of yourself, you must learn to expect your dysfunctional parts to pop up so that you can continue to find ways to challenge yourself to make new decisions. And these new decisions should be consistent with your new values and your newly defined boundaries. Reset yourself and keep moving forward every time you mess up.

Choosing the right people today will also require you to set some standards for what you are looking for. Standards will vary, depending on your age and where you are in your life, as well as your future ambitions. For some people, just having a penis or a vagina will do, as sex itself is most important. Sex may always be important to you, and you'll build on that with things like kindness, consideration, thoughtfulness, being employed, being educated, having good credit, not being a felon, suffering no addiction, paying bills, and overall, having one's shit together. Refer to the values list you created earlier and add to that list the standards based on your individual needs; make revisions as you identify newly defined values and boundaries. This relationship you're building with yourself is the most important one, and you must always remember to avoid losing sight of yourself because, the moment that you do, everything that you've worked for will fall apart. Once you've done all of the groundwork, you can start looking for potential partners, and as soon as you find someone you're attracted to immediately, become friends first.

Being friends with someone helps you to get to know them without the pressure of having to rush things into a commitment, like saying "I do." But most importantly, friendship is the foundation for healthy romantic relationships. Friendship also allows for an appropriate pace and gives you a chance to walk consciously into love rather than falling blindly into it, as if you're falling into a black hole.

Jumping into a romantic relationship may also trigger your "good enough" wounds. *Do they think I am good enough? Am I pretty enough? Strong enough? Tall enough? Skinny enough?* Every time you entertain your insecurities, you'll be forced out of the present moment to tend to those thoughts, and everything related to getting to know this person will be put on hold. Friendship allows for acceptance, though—first of who you are and then of who they are. When you're busy entertaining your insecurities, you'll also be focused on becoming who you think the other person wants you to be instead of just being your amazing self. So, stay focused on being grounded and just observe your behaviors, as well as your feelings, and pay attention to your triggers while also absorbing what you are learning about the other person. Allow yourself to stay present and enjoy the moments that feel great while continuing to get to know them.

Friendship gives you a space from which to assess the other person without the pressure of needing to make an immediate decision about them romantically. Ideally, during this time, you will also want to avoid having sex even if you move beyond the friendship stage, as the risk of having sex too soon is the creation of premature attachments. Sex releases endorphins that your brain loves, and those endorphins can become addicting, which will then become distracting. These distractions then blindfold you to the potential of red flags, and so for these reasons, if you can, avoid sex at first. Let the tension build; thank me later.

Allowing love to evolve slowly gives you permission to talk about things that make you feel uncomfortable, causing you to practice stating and sometimes restating your boundaries. When boundaries are crossed and you say something, how does the other person respond? How do you feel internally from doing it? Pay attention to these things. Paying attention leads to understanding a person's true character before committing your entire heart based on chemistry alone. Chemistry is amazing, but without compatibility, it is not enough to sustain a committed and healthy relationship.

Identifying Red Flags

As you become healthier, you'll be better able to identify red flags, but being raised in a dysfunctional environment may make it hard for you to see them in advance. So let's take some time to look at important red flags which you can't afford to miss. Use the below examples to help you get started with creating your own list, as red flags vary.

1. Abusive Behavior: Abuse is not always obvious, and it never starts out that way, but if you see it at all, it is best for you to end the relationship and walk away immediately. Abuse can be either emotional or physical, and both types are equally damaging. Name-calling, belittling, and humiliation are all forms of emotional abuse, while pushing, grabbing, choking, and slapping are examples of physical abuse. Abuse can also be sexual, and just because you are in a relationship does not mean that you should participate in anything that ever makes you feel uncomfortable. You can say "no," even if you are married.

   Since abuse does not usually show up right away, pacing a relationship is extremely helpful. Early warning signs include the way your partner treats other people or talks about other people, including those closest to them, so pay attention to how they speak about their family and look for ways that they take accountability for their current relationships. Blaming others for their circumstances should highlight that they are not capable of taking responsibility for the way things are in their life.
2. Communication Problems: Healthy communication involves being able to consider each person's thoughts and feelings in a non-threatening way. A

person's inability to express themselves will lead to additional problems later on; when people cannot use their words to communicate, they'll use reaction-seeking behavior instead. Reaction-seeking behavior is manipulative and leaves the focus of such behavior feeling confused. Persistent feelings of guilt or confusion are your clues that something is very wrong. If you are unable to talk about an issue with your partner, then there is little hope that things will ever improve, and they're likely to only continue to worsen. Communication must be important to both partners if a relationship is going to be healthy, and it must be encouraged often.

3. Insecurity: Insecurity is a red flag because it signals an inner battle that cannot be won via external forces. If the person does not see the value that they hold, then they will not be able to receive validation from you. If they do not believe that they are attractive, then a million compliments will not resonate, which may then cause you to doubt yourself. If you find yourself starting to question your own value, then that is your sign that there are serious problems.
4. Immaturity, Instability, and Unpredictability: These are red flags because they contribute to conflict in relationships through behaviors like poor impulse control, jealousy, rageful outbursts, egotistical pride, entitlement, blame, and a need to try to control others. If you cannot bring these issues up without the

other person becoming inflamed, they will likely escalate into more abusive patterns.

5. A Dark or Secretive Past: I will always encourage you to allow people to be who they are today and not box them into the corner of who they used to be, but having an understanding of your partner's past will help you be aware of possible future behaviors. Things that are important to know are their history of cheating or being abusive, any addictions (past or present), and legal history. When you are seriously considering a future with someone, having a solid understanding of their past will help you make a wise decision.

These are my top five red flags which I'd suggest you look out for in order to avoid a damaging and toxic relationship, but I also encourage you to add to this list and create your own to continue defining and improving your standards. Standards, values, and boundaries around particular behaviors serve as protection for your heart and your mind, as far too many of you know just how hard it is to fully recover from a toxic relationship. Toxic relationships destroy your sense of self, leaving you to pick up all of your broken pieces and rebuild again. Instead, you have to allow yourself to learn from the hurts of your past, or you will run the risk of repeating them. It is okay if you chose someone who turned out to be unhealthy, as you can't know these things right off the bat, but know when to walk away. Remember, most people show up as the best version of themselves for at least the first six months of a relationship. Pacing a relationship will allow you to see if their persona is an act before you're too involved, and if it is an act, then it will not be sustainable. The real objective here is for you to learn to practice staying grounded and enforcing your boundaries rather than abandoning yourself.

Managing conflict in your relationship will be the next area of focus we tackle, as the presence or absence of conflict is not an accurate measure of healthiness—everyone experiences conflict, after all. An important thing to know about conflict is that it can't always be resolved, and so learning how to effectively manage it is an important skill. The most important skill for managing conflict in a relationship is based in your ability to manage conflict within you. Managing inner conflict and awareness that recognizes when your brain is flooded is helpful in conflict management. Flooding causes your brain to stop rationalizing and to react in one of the following ways: fight-flight, freeze, or fawn/flop. Self-awareness will help you to receive the signals that your body sends you to let you know that you are getting flooded. If you have a hard time connecting to your body, consider investing in an activity monitor, as that can provide a tremendous amount of insight into how you are feeling. Having an activity tracker is helpful because of its quick access to your pulse—90 beats or more per minute, and you're heading into the danger zone! Giving yourself room to take a time-out and decompress before talking about difficult things can help you avoid arguments. Your brain needs about a half-hour to regulate itself, so pay attention to each other and notice how the other person is receiving information. That way, you can create a safe place by saying things like, "I am getting upset" or "I can see that you're getting upset, so let's take a break"—and then you can try talking about the issue again in an hour, a day, or whenever, as long as you define the time. Defining the time also helps you feel confident that things will not just be swept under the rug and never talked about again, which is something that many couples fear.

When managing difficult conversations, be sure that you stick to how something has made you feel instead of telling the other person how they feel. You will never be able to tell someone what they are feeling, but rather, you need to acknowledge that you are each having your own unique experience and you must leave room for that reality. Use "I feel" statements instead of "you make me feel" statements. Take ownership of your feelings, and always check for understanding. Being able to view a situation from the other person's perspective is called *empathy*.

Empathy means understanding what your partner feels; it is not taking responsibility for the other person's feelings. Validate each other's feelings and take ownership of your behaviors—because you can only ever control yourself. Your partner is not wrong for feeling the way they do, and how you handle their feelings will help or hurt the outcome.

Avoid criticism or saying things like "You are too sensitive" because that will lead to a person shutting down or becoming defensive. Ideally, we want to encourage each other to be open and honest about the way we feel and not make anyone feel bad for it. If you are having a hard time understanding how your partner feels, then stick to sympathy and validating while considering their perspective; and if you realize that you've contributed to the negative sentiment in some way, apologize. You may unintentionally hurt each other's feelings by not having the necessary insight at the time, so being able to apologize for being wrong is not a sign of weakness, but an opportunity for growth. Teachable moments are blessings in disguise. Give each other time to process and resolve negative emotions, as everyone processes things differently, and some people move along faster than others—neither path is right or wrong. It is possible for someone, especially men, to need days to process an incident or conversation. Healthy relationships are focused on feeling seen and being heard and not on who is right or wrong. If winning is the focus of a partnership, then you are both losers in the relationship.

Turning toward your partner and listening to what's being said is another crucial skill. All too often, we listen only to respond to our own interpretation of what is being said, thus missing the whole thing altogether. Active listening promotes connections by encouraging you to seek understanding; ask for clarification, paraphrasing what you have heard, and notice non-verbal body language like facial expressions. Listening for understanding requires our full attention, as you want your partner to feel cared about, and turning toward them conveys that message. When you listen actively for understanding, you will not be attaching personally to what is being said because you'll be allowing your partner to have a negative experience without making it about yourself. When listening, you may find that the helper in you will want to make things better for your partner, and that may not be what they need in the here and now. Couples work has been shown to have a trend of one common complaint: "They are always telling me how to fix it, but I don't want to fix it right now—I just need to talk about it." Most people have the answers to their problems and know what they need to do, but they still want to get it off their chest, so give them space for that. Allowing someone to vent is easy and only requires your presence and attention. Paying attention to what is being said and then imagining how that might make you feel is an opportunity for you to exercise empathy. Sometimes the only words that you will have to say are things like "That sucks," and that will be exactly what it takes to help your partner feel validated and heard. If you're in a place where you're not sure what your partner needs from you in a given moment, just ask them, "How can I best support you with this?" The more open-ended questions you ask, the stronger the communication in your relationship will be.

Love Languages and Knowing What Your Partner Needs

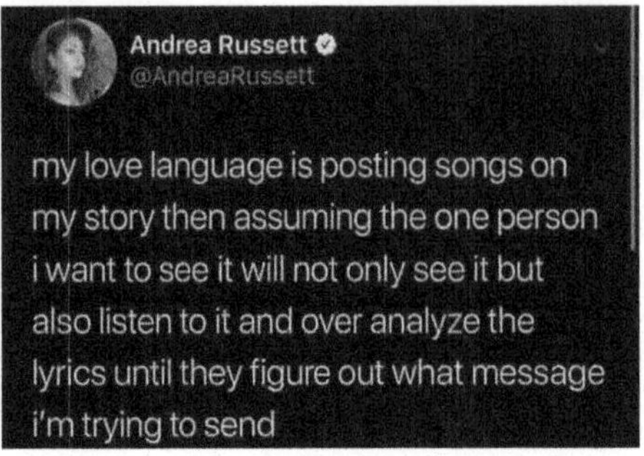

As you continue to build a foundation for your relationship—one rooted in listening and communicating—you'll also be pouring a solid foundation to build a healthy future together. With more stability in the foundation, you will feel safe exploring each other's love languages and getting to know one another more deeply. Love languages give you more perspective on what your partner needs to feel loved. There are fun and free online quizzes that you can take to learn each other's love languages. In his book, *The 5 Love Languages*, Gary Chapman[11] defines them as words of affirmation, acts of service, and receiving gifts, quality time, and physical touch.

For people who feel love with words of affirmation, providing compliments and appreciation go a long way. Pay attention to your partner's hair or clothes, and offer a little praise to connect to their hearts. Those who believe love is action over words will need you to do things for them; consider ways that you can help with dishes, laundry, or cooking, as helping ease

11 Gary Chapman ***The 5 Love Languages: The Secret to Love that Lasts***

life's endless chores is love. A person who focuses on receiving gifts may cause you to think that they're materialistic, but know that it's the thought that counts here. It can be the smallest gesture that resonates the most—like bringing home their favorite candy bar, for example. Quality time means just that; a person with this focus wants you to spend time with them! This can be hard when people are juggling so many responsibilities and have such limited time, so if this is your love language, be realistic with your expectations of how much time you'll be able to receive. For example, if your partner chooses to go to the gym instead of spending time with you, remember that they are to fill their own cup before being able to pour anything into yours. Be sure that you are also spending quality time in other relationships, like with your friends or family, to lessen your partner's responsibility. Those who connect love with a physical touch need you to hold their hand, offer hugs and kisses, touch, feel, and have sex; without the physical connection, they will often feel rejected. So, be mindful of putting your hand on your partner's shoulder, caressing their face, and playing with their hair to fill their love buckets.

Banking on Love

Once you define what the other person's needs are, then you can set up your relationship's emotional bank account. Each one of you should be charged with making deposits and not just withdrawals. This is what people mean when they say that relationships take work—this is the work: wanting to know who your partner truly is and wanting to understand what their needs are, and then wanting to meet their needs. When a person feels like they have to do this work instead of wanting to do it, that's when the relationship becomes "hard work." If you don't want to learn to consider the other person, then it will feel forced. Love should never be forced, and it is not controlled; it is accepting and reciprocal.

You will need lots of consistency and stability to strengthen trust and deepen the level of commitment. Transitioning to a "we" mentality from a "me" mentality requires readjusting and reprioritizing your lives. By the time you reach this point in a relationship, you will have shared your values, and together you can create a shared value system that best represents both of you. This value system tells each of you how to represent the relationship even when you are apart. A healthy relationship enhances and adds value to your life; your ideal partner is a person you can lean on to support you and the goals you have for yourself and each other. Your partner should encourage you to try new things, celebrate your passions, support you during your lows, and offer you a place to rest safely without judgment or criticism. They should ground you when life has you feeling restless, and that's the type of culture you want to create in your relationship so that you'll have everything you need to make it stand up to the tests of time. Time brings lots of new challenges for relationships—like children, illnesses, job loss, financial problems, aging parents, and grandchildren, to name a few. If you take the time to define what you both represent, you'll be able to overcome problems by enforcing the principles and values that keep you together.

Managing Stress Together

My wife got in her gym clothes, delivered an angry five-minute rant about how much she loves bread, then started cry-laughing at an unintelligible joke she mumbled between hysterical sobs.

I have never been so scared in my life.

Marriages and long-term committed relationships will face many hardships, and this is when it will be important to remember that you're each going to have different responses to the circumstances—and neither one of you is necessarily right nor wrong. Stressors will attempt to divide you, and it is your responsibility to not lose sight of the relationship when you are going through those difficulties, but that can be really hard. Maybe your spouse loses their job, and you weren't prepared for the financial strain, so this creates an opportunity for both of you to feel a negative emotion related to the job loss. Since each of you is having your own unique experience, you must remember to acknowledge and validate each other and always turn back toward one another to develop the strategy for managing current stressors together. Your relationship mantra: "It is you and me, not you vs. me." Stressors will negatively impact your mental health, and your mood will affect your behaviors, so be mindful of taking care of yourselves during life's difficulties and reminding each other of the same. Always keep practicing your grounding skills to soothe yourself and each other by exhibiting that energy to your partner, who will also need it.

Not all stressors in relationships are negative, of course—some are positive, like having children or getting a promotion, as both can bring major changes to your lives. Conversations around expectations are necessary for staying connected, so do not forget your relationship bank account while adjusting to the new normal, and continue to make your deposits without losing sight of each other. There are so many things bidding for your attention these days, so you need to be very intentional about making deposits to the love bank account or run the risk of it running in the negative.

One stressor of adjusting to life as new parents is its impact on your sex life. Sometimes, you will stop having sex before the baby even arrives because Mom does not feel well or isn't in the mood. Resist bottling up resentment and encourage talking to each other about ways to compromise and be understanding. It is common to have conflict when adjusting to parenting, especially with your first child when you are both feeling a lot of pressure and fear about doing things right or wrong. Do yourself a favor and sit down to talk about your expectations because raising a child is physically and emotionally taxing. Once there's a new baby around, you're not eating well, you're probably not sleeping well, and maybe you've even given up your workout routine because it feels like you don't have time or you're simply too tired. Acknowledging that you are both maxed out will help you to avoid turning on each other. Again, always keep in mind that each of you is having a unique experience and managing your emotions in your own ways. Create structure and routine around childcare, work, and alone time, and encourage each other to follow it. Your relationship mantra here: "A good me makes a better we." Adopt this mindset to encourage each other to practice good self-care, which will lead to optimal mental health.

Differences in parenting styles will also bring conflict into a new family, so make sure to try hearing each other out and practicing your listening skills. There will probably also be outside influences giving you tips and suggestions on how to create a perfect family, but it is important that you try to minimize the outside noise and focus on finding common ground between each other. You are allowed to create a system that works for your new family and is based on your shared values. Allowing outside influences too much power will increase the conflict between you, so you need to establish boundaries and enforce them to protect your relationship and your new family. You have done so much work in creating a system for your relationship that it's important to always consider each other first. Without the system in place and without structure, you'll only lead yourselves to a collapse.

The Hard Goodbyes

Michael Adler
@madler9000

Just settled a divorce over visitation of a parrot. Neither may teach it negative phrases about the other. I went to law school for this.

Despite all of the best intentions, many relationships will fail, and more than half of all marriages end in divorce. Let us look at what causes relationships to break down and how to know if yours is over. The standards and boundaries you took the time to create will also serve as guides for your absolute dealbreakers. Everyone needs to know their own rules for where they draw the line; for some, it's infidelity, and for others, it's lying. For everyone, a dealbreaker should be abuse. Abuse of any kind is a dealbreaker to establish for yourself, as it is impossible to recover once those boundaries have been broken. When your safety is compromised, your trust in that person will be obliterated. If they are capable of hurting you physically or emotionally, then they are incapable of protecting you, and your only option is to leave. Other factors that lead to relationship failure include the following:

Not having your needs met
Neglect
Apathy

Constant fighting
Addiction
Feeling like roommates
Lack of communication
Walking on eggshells
Decline in mental or physical health

Your first clue that a relationship is not healthy is how you are feeling mentally and physically. A bad relationship will have you feeling depressed and anxious; it will leave you with migraine headaches, stomach aches, and chronic fatigue. Separation at this stage is helpful in allowing yourself to regulate and make the next decision from a state of wellness rather than illness. Give each other space to take a step back, regroup, and regain perspective. People always worry about not having a good enough reason to leave, so let your wellness or lack thereof be your guide, and it will always steer you in the right direction. You are allowed to walk away from anything that is compromising your health. Apathy is another clear indicator of the end of a relationship; apathy comes when neither one of you cares about what happens anymore—and you do not want to care, either. When you get to this place, there is truly little hope that both of you will be able to view your relationship through a positive lens again. When apathy is allowed to build up, it changes the way you view each other so that instead of believing the best, you only see the worst—and the layers of negativity you feel toward the other will continue to pile up. When couples come to counseling, the first thing I ask myself is whether they are a couple who doesn't want to do the work—or a couple who doesn't know how to do the work. If they are willing to learn, then they can get their relationship back on track. Working on the relationship will require both of them to take ownership and accountability for their roles in the breakdown of their relationship.

Getting to a place of wellness will help you when you are struggling to make a stay-or-go decision. When you are well, you can rationalize and see things for what they really are. If it is the end, as much as it'll hurt, you'll be able to see that and view it as the best option for both of you. Even your children will be better off in separate households if it means access to two healthy parents. Staying in a toxic environment means passing down that torch to your children, only to have them then recreate a life filled with the same dysfunction. Break the curse passed down to you by choosing to glow up into the best version of you, even if that means being alone.

Moving on from divorce or a major breakup is a painful process filled with so much grief. Give yourself all the time you need to fully process everything associated with this loss. Loss is painful even if a relationship was toxic. You are going to hurt because you loved your partner and formed an attachment to them, and detaching from someone is excruciating. Be patient with yourself, as there is no time line for grief; you will move on only when you've gone through the entire process. Compassion and kindness toward yourself will also help you to move forward, as blame and shame will only keep you stuck replaying all of the things you *coulda woulda shoulda* done differently. Forgiving yourself will also help you heal, and then, when you realize the ways you went wrong, you'll learn something new. Because of that relationship experience, you can have gratitude for the lesson because you've fully grieved the loss. As the great Maya Angelou said, "When you know better, you do better." Always remember that you are a continual work in progress, so let go of your mistakes and move forward, better able to avoid them in the future. Forgiveness restores the relationship you have with yourself, and when you trust yourself, you will try again—this time, as a better version of you. Allow the higher versions of you to constantly develop and show up in your current and future relationships. This will allow you to create the love you truly desire with a full understanding of what love is and what it isn't. You're deserving of that kind of love.

Part 4: Healing and Accessing Better Versions of You

Hope Carpenter
@hopepriestess

Don't rush Grief out the door. Invite her in for tea and take notes. She has much to teach you.

Healing allows for defining moments, and those will help you access better versions of yourself; each version increases your self-awareness. Healing involves honoring all of the past versions of you—including the good, the bad, and the indifferent. It is through this intentional process of validating each part of us and our experiences that we heal. During this process, we will encounter parts of ourselves that have been locked away in our hopes of forgetting, but memories will be triggered, and pieces will start to become clearer. When healing work reveals those fragmented parts of us, seeing them for the first time can be significantly distressing, or in other words, it's scary. It's always useful to work with a therapist when you decide to embark on this journey because they have access to and will share a wealth of tools and resources to help you learn to regulate yourself in times of distress during the healing process. The healing process brings layers of grief, and learning to sit with grief is what you need to do in order to stay well when things aren't.

The brain constructs memories through time traveling and never really knows the difference between fantasy and reality; that's why people aren't really sure if what happened to them actually happened to them or if they're making it up. When you're struggling to discern between fantasy and reality, focus on the feelings attached to your memories and validate those instead of trying to piece the story together. The unvalidated feelings will lead to emotional flashbacks later, as unprocessed trauma allows old feelings to hijack the present moment. As feelings come up during memory recall, it's important to validate and express them; this is how we are able to let go. Old feelings and emotions that remain locked away will impact the here and now, as well as the future too.

In honoring the past versions of ourselves, we grieve the experiences that hurt them, and grief allows those wounded parts to feel heard, seen, and accepted. They now know that what happened to them was not okay and that they are allowed to feel sad, angry, rageful, all of it because the adult you are today can hold the space for the pain of the past. Trauma survivors have often had their experiences and emotions completely minimized. They've been told that it didn't really happen, that it was their fault, or that someone else has it worse—in other words, to JUST GET OVER IT! Yet, getting over it requires passing through all of the emotions, or else they'll resurface elsewhere as emotional or physical flashbacks. As we talked about in relation to trauma and coping mechanisms, a wounded part of yourself that has experienced severe trauma, humiliation, or embarrassment has been disconnected from the self, never to be heard from again because of the pain it represents. Connecting to your wounded parts involves accessing your inner child, children, or other wounded part. This is hard for some people and easier for others, depending on how detached they are from their past selves.

Self-Exploration Exercise:

A helpful exercise to facilitate the connection to your wounded parts comes via the use of pictures. Go look for pictures of you from as far back as you can find and observe each photo carefully while looking for the story within. Look at your eyes, facial expressions, and body language, and ask yourself, what are they telling you? Can you identify any emotions? Is there sadness, confusion, or happiness to be seen? While you're going through these photos, take the time to create a timeline for yourself and write down any significant moments, including the traumatic moments, that may come to mind throughout this exercise. This would also be a good time to pick up a journal and write out each of those stories as they come to you, in exactly the way that you remember them. As you write, imagine what you were feeling and write down those feelings, too. Pay attention to how your body feels when those feelings come. Look for energy, and consider, where do you feel the emotions? Connecting back to your body and paying attention to what's happening internally will tell you a lot about the story you are trying to remember, as the body holds many secrets. Dial up the love here and connect with all those faces, all those past versions of you with compassion.

Don't be afraid of what you're feeling, and remind yourself often that you're safe now. Visualize yourself as the strong adult you are today, protecting that child you used to be, and extend your hand out to that child—letting them know that they are protected and not alone.

Shame, the Worst Feeling Ever

Sometimes it's not the memories that scare us, but the feelings that come along with them—like shame. Shame will cause us to run away every time, which is why leading with forgiveness is so vital to this process. Shame tells you a story about you deserving whatever you're going through because what happened was your fault. If you hear that inner dialogue, though, snap your fingers or clap your hands; these are thought-stopping techniques to shut it down. Don't turn away from yourself when you reach this place; instead, dial up the self-compassion you need in order to seek the why behind the choices you felt you needed to make during those times. Authenticity is achieved through acceptance of the self, despite anything that has happened in the past. It's a decision to no longer be controlled by what other people might think or posture to only reveal the parts of you that you know will be liked and accepted. As you put the pieces of the puzzle that is your life together, you may see that there were no other options within your reach during your most cringe-worthy memories. I encourage you to push through those feelings and keep pressing on, remembering that what you did then doesn't need to be attached to who you are today. My clients will sometimes tell me that if I knew who they were, I wouldn't like them, and they say that because they associate old behaviors with who they are today without allowing themselves the freedom that comes with letting go and experiencing growth. Be focused on who you are *today*.

Be more protective of yourself by asserting that your choices were the best you could do at that time, and given another opportunity, maybe the experience could look different based on what you now know today. Brené Brown, an amazing researcher on the subject of shame and vulnerability, defines shame as an intensely painful feeling or experience of believing that we are flawed and, therefore, unworthy of love and belonging. In her work, she describes "shame shields" as the three primary responses to shame: moving away from it, moving toward it, and moving against it. (Brown, 2020) To move toward shame is to become a people-pleaser first and foremost, to create a distance between you and your shame being discovered. It's a sweaty pursuit of perfection to mask the shame. Moving away is to retreat and isolate yourself from others to prevent your shame from being discovered. Finally, moving against shame is to react toward it aggressively and to fight back, hurting anyone who gets too close to your shame by inflicting pain on them either physically or emotionally. In our malignant management of shame, we lose connections to others due to the fear of revealing our true selves or the risk of being exposed, but it's with this very risk that we become vulnerable and real. Freeing yourself from the prison of shame takes great courage and will create acceptance of the real, perfectly imperfect you.

Working through shame requires compassion and sensitivity, as it leaves you feeling raw and afraid. But if you stick with it as it falls away, your worth and value will be restored and revealed. In building worth and value, we begin to see how we were always deserving of having our experiences validated even if there has been no one capable of doing it for us in the past. This is a good opportunity to consider therapy because the therapeutic relationship provides the safety and security for you to process grief without judgment or criticism. A skilled helper will be able to show you how to see yourself through a new lens and show you what's been missing inside of you all along—belief. Having this safe place to share your timeline, traumas, journals, and experiences can make all the difference. You'll be met with different and sometimes intense feelings in this process, so having someone there to guide you through them is crucial in properly processing everything. A skilled helper offers empathy, as well, which minimizes shame by helping a person know that they are not alone and not at fault. When you disarm the shame, you rescue the wounded part of yourself that's been imprisoned, rescuing that part of you from what you did or what happened. As the shame decreases, the empathy increases, so the more validated you'll feel; with increased validation also comes decreased blame. Blame is also responsible for keeping you quiet, but now you'll be free to love yourself through the different stages of grief and allow yourself to reach acceptance and finally let go.

Grief is an important part of this process, and you grieve what has happened in order to release the trapped emotions that are interfering with your quality of life today. Grieving is an uncomfortable and continuous process, and you'll find that some experiences will always bring you some feeling of grief no matter how many times you've looked at it. Always make room for the feelings, as uncomfortable as they may be; while to grieve may bring suffering, to truly suffer is to not acknowledge all the losses and the pain that came with them.

Accessing your emotions will feel overwhelming at times, especially when it comes to those that you didn't even know you had. As you talk through your experiences in a therapeutic setting, you will be afforded the opportunity to see how the past is causing you to behave in ways that are impacting your current relationships. Sometimes, through this process, you'll begin to question some of your current relationships, especially if you're in a relationship with people who have hurt you, and you're only coming to realize that today. As a result of what you're feeling, you might want to take some of the frustration out on the ones that hurt you. Be aware that, in some cases, when confronted, an abusive person will completely deny the allegations—making you feel crazy and making confrontation a risky choice. In all of your relationships going forward, you will have to define or redefine boundaries and assert yourself when others cross them. As uncomfortable as those conversations are, they are completely necessary for helping you to stay mentally well. Because your support system is so incredibly important to your mental health, there may even come a time where you'll need to cut someone out of your life completely because they've violated your boundaries, and when you start to love yourself fully, you'll be more protective and less tolerant of abusive behaviors. Consider adopting this mantra: "I will not sign up for abuse as an adult."

Closure

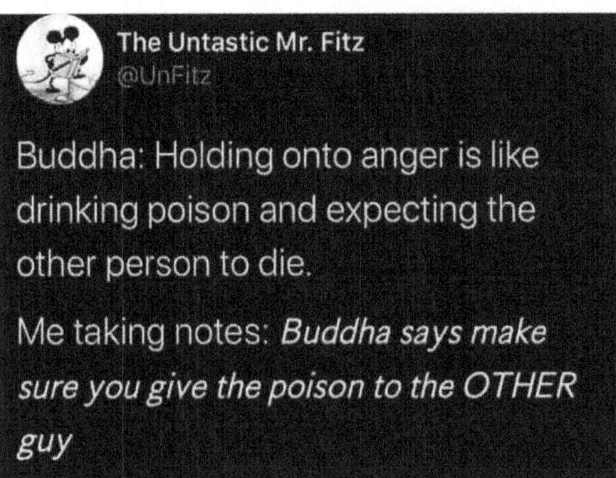

It's normal to want closure, as closure gives you a chance to speak your mind and let someone know how they've made you feel. Many times, people want closure to move forward, but conversations with those responsible for the pain that you're in may be impossible for whatever reason, so there are other ways that you can go about gaining closure in a therapeutic setting. An effective strategy for releasing the inner feelings you have toward someone is through the process of letter writing, where you allow yourself to write a letter saying whatever it is you need to say to whoever hurt you, telling them how you feel in whatever language is effective. Make it as strong as necessary for you to feel like you're standing up for and defending yourself. You can say whatever you'd like. Tell them to fuck off. Say it out loud. Shout it! FUCK OFF, (insert name here)! Once you're done writing, you can role-play in therapy, allowing yourself to speak those words out loud to someone who will validate your feelings, or you can place a picture of that person on a chair across the room from you and read the letter aloud, which is similar to the empty chair technique commonly used in Gestalt therapy. Once you've fully expressed your feelings, you can choose to burn the letter in a ceremony, allowing the ashes to symbolize that you're letting go so that you can then blow those ashes away. This is an extremely cathartic experience and an exercise that I encourage you to participate in, as letting go leads to healing and mental wellness.

The letting go process is completely meant for you personally; you don't have to share it with anyone. It's you giving yourself permission to no longer carry around the pain inflicted on you and no longer allow it to negatively color your world. Letting go doesn't mean forgetting—and it doesn't mean forgiving, either, as some people have hurt you so badly that they don't deserve your forgiveness. But you can still let go of the pain that they've caused you.

Since time doesn't necessarily heal all wounds, expect grief to visit from time to time. When it shows up, acknowledge its presence, look for the emotions that it's bringing, and find healthy and effective ways to express them. When sadness visits, you may need to cry. When anger shows up, you may need to write, take a cold shower, or run. Finding useful ways to emote can be learned with a therapist. They can prepare you for the tidal waves of sadness that will sometimes come when you think of the losses of your childhood or relationships or the pain of unmet expectations. Allow yourself to cry, and let the tears flow no matter how much you've been conditioned to view crying as a weakness, as the ability to release tears is very much a strength.

For those who struggle to induce tears, I encourage you to look for movies, listen to music, or watch videos that will encourage their flow. You can also expect to feel lots of anger. Know that anger is a normal human emotion. You're allowed to be angry; you're even allowed to be *outraged* at what you've been through, and how you express those feelings will define you. Just remember that impulsive behaviors can have catastrophic consequences. It's never helpful to take anger out on yourself or others. Some effective ways of expressing anger include activities that activate adrenaline, putting to good use that energy coming from your nervous system. Not having good strategies in place for the management of intense emotions sets you up for checking out of the present moment through a process called disassociation.

Dissociation and Emotional Flashbacks

Connecting to and coming back home to your body is achieved through learning ways of grounding yourself. Staying present means learning the most effective ways to regulate your emotions and prevent dissociative responses. There will be moments on this journey where your healing will be interrupted, and you will feel triggered, leading to intense sensations running through your body that you must learn to identify to bring yourself back to a stable place. Dissociation involves feeling disconnected from yourself, your body, and the present moment; it often happens to those who have a history of trauma. Many people don't even know they're doing it, let alone why. It occurs when the present moment becomes emotionally or physically unbearable, to the extent that checking out of the present moment is the only safe option. In severe cases, people will suffer from mental illnesses like depersonalization/derealization disorder, dissociative identity disorder, or dissociative amnesia.

What does it look like? Dissociative states may look like someone is spaced out, daydreaming, or exhibiting a blank stare on their face. Other times, it's an impulsive and often extreme physical reaction or radical shift in a person's mood, also known as an emotional flashback.

Emotional flashbacks are intensely disturbing regressions to the overwhelming feeling-states of your childhood abandonment. When you are stuck in a flashback, fear, shame, and/or depression can dominate your experience.[12] Those of you on the healing path right now need to understand that there are going to be times when, intellectually, you'll know it's happening, and because you can't stop it, you'll feel significant distress, but keep going, and you'll get better. We are not looking for perfection, just continued progress. The reason you can't stop it completely is that there is no way to be able to predict all of the emotional landmines that this journey of life will hide from you. Knowing what to do when flashbacks happen means allowing yourself to be present now—because you know how to anchor yourself when those storms come, and this knowledge will help you to weather them.

As you learn to identify when you're dissociating or having an emotional flashback, you may identify patterns with their appearances and the reasons for the stormy seasons will become more predictable, as you'll understand the triggers—such as visiting your family, meeting with your boss, or being in a large, crowded setting. Any time you have to engage in related activities, you can prepare yourself emotionally by putting proper boundaries in place. It's those unknown landmines that are tricky, like living through this pandemic brought to us by COVID-19. This pandemic is causing a significant and rapid decline in mental health for many people,

12 (Walker, p. 145)

as their brains are going through rapid cycling of thoughts and emotions in attempting to create a blueprint for pandemics. Since most of us have never had our lives involuntarily canceled, our brains don't have a neural pathway for this experience figured out just yet. While we may have chosen not to participate in life for whatever reasons in the past, to be sheltering in place, social distancing, wearing masks, and having no time frame on these restrictions is a massive source of distress. The limbic system that we talked about earlier is sensing danger, and as we've covered earlier, that gets your brain stuck in a state of hypervigilance, causing you to respond in a flight, fight, freeze, or fawn response. Living in this heightened state causes our adrenal system to pump out hormones that, when sent into overload, leave us feeling panicky, sensitive, fearful, and exhausted. This pandemic is a traumatic event, which means we are all traumatized and, as a result, all need to learn how to regulate our minds and bodies to survive. The dissociative techniques for survival that are most often being peddled to all of us through memes today are the encouragement to drink ourselves into a coma on a daily basis or to eat 50,000 calories by noon, neither of which is recommended. The best pandemic blueprint that you can draw must have very specific plans for the day-to-day details. Boundaries on time, food, hydration, sleep, technology, work, etc., need to have defined measurables that contribute to you feeling your best. While you're at it, be honest with yourself about the things that make you feel like shit right now. What are the activities that you're practicing, who are the people that you're surrounding yourself with that are contributing to bad vibes, and what choices do you have here?

Neurofeedback and Your Automatic Nervous System

What is recommended is having a working understanding of your brain and your nervous system more deeply to help yourself stay present, talk yourself through the difficult moments, and avoid disassociating. Many new and fascinating ways to study our brains are helping us learn more about them and how certain brain wave production in excess can increase anxiety symptoms. Having my brain mapped for a fascinating technique called neurofeedback showed that my brain produced excess high beta waves, which are responsible for impulsivity and anxiety. After 60 sessions of neurofeedback training, my beta waves were reduced by over 50 percent, thus reducing my symptoms. Neurofeedback uses sensors to measure electrical activity and is regulated through the use of sight and sound. By wearing a device on my head, I saw the changes to my brain waves when I was clenching my teeth or scrunching my forehead, as the system would send me a feedback signal telling me to stop moving so much to help me focus. With it forcing me to pay attention to the tension in my body, I was able to relax and improve my attention span. The skills I learned from these feedback sessions are skills that I now use when I'm coaching others to help raise their awareness around tension in their bodies. This is helpful evidence of an effective treatment that proves our brains are always capable of learning, which changes how we feel.

The important thing to know about our nervous system is that it's a communication center made up of the brain, the spinal cord, and the nerves. When there's a danger perceived, it sounds warning signals—like the feeling you get when you turn out the lights and hear something in your closet; that paralyzing fear that comes over you is your autonomic nervous system being fired up—your personal neighborhood watch, if you will. It's composed of two distinct features: the sympathetic, which prepares the body for intensity by activating fight or flight response, and the parasympathetic, which relaxes and slows the body down. *Autonomic* means that we don't have to do anything to cause something to happen, like breathing. You don't have to think about breathing; it just happens. The most fascinating part of it is the research emerging, which suggests that if we stop to consciously focus on things like our breath, we could also control our minds and our bodies. To understand the depth of this power, let me also tell you about a superhuman, Wim Hof, also known as "the Ice Man." He developed a method that overrides the autonomic nervous system and controls the mind; the Wim Hof Method is based on three pillars: cold therapy (which is known to enhance the body's ability to boost its mood), breathing, and commitment. Ice and cold are commonly used in therapy to regulate intense feelings, and his method takes this to a whole new level. In an interview, he shared that the urge to jump into freezing water came as a way for him to cope with the suicide of his first wife. His emotional pain was so incredibly intense that "mercilessly cold water" was the cure for soothing it.[13] This serves as an example of how pain will serve a purpose, and that purpose may be bigger than you've ever imagined.

Coming Back to the Present Moment through Heart Rate Variability

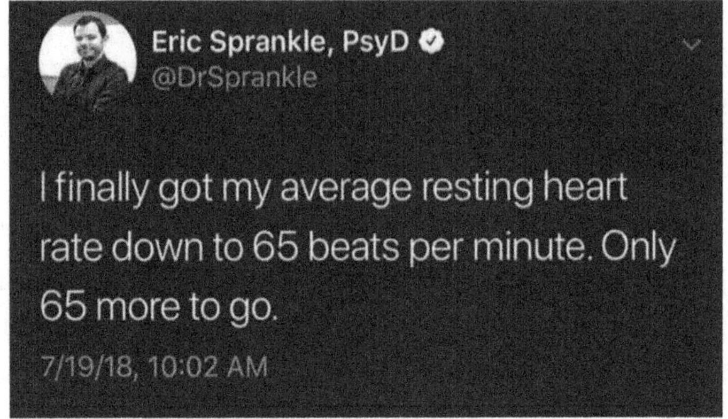

If escaping pain is what disassociation is all about, then tolerating the grief it brings in the moment is truly the only way to endure and heal it. This is the time to learn how to sit with grief and then how to effectively express it. If you didn't have any emotional pain before, today's headlines are full of it, as COVID-19 has certainly dropped some off at your doorstep. It's the ups and the downs that are hard to deal with; one day, you're feeling safe inside of your bubble, practicing all of the self-care like walking and eating right, and the next moment, you're looking for substances to numb the pain, to

13 Vice Documentary: The Superhuman World of Wim Hof: The Ice Man

stop your crying, to get you through the moment, and help you survive. If you find yourself vacillating between extremes, please know that you're not alone, and continue committing to learning new skills to help you practice self-control during the moments that feel the most out of control. Sometimes, getting through just one minute at a time is the best that we can do. The skills that I keep referring to are literally any technique that allows you to feel grounded and aware of the here and now rather than being lost in the filing cabinets of your mind. It's the ability to feel calmness in your body, to be still, to ease a racing heart, and to soothe yourself to inner peace.

At the center of all these different techniques is the constant need to monitor your breathing and learn about heart rate variability. Do you know how to take your heart rate? Are you able to find your pulse? What's the number? What does it mean? The average resting heart rate is between 60 and 80 BPM (beats per minute). The better the physical shape that you're in, the lower your BPM will be. Some athletes have a BPM as low as 30, and the lower your BPM is, the more relaxed a state your body is able to fall into. Pay attention to your heart rate when you're around different people and in different environments, and learn how to connect back to your body so that you can understand when it's not in a good place and how to restore it to a regulated state. When your heart is at 90 BPM or more, your brain will become flooded, which means your ability to rationalize will decrease while you engage in fight, flight, freeze, or fawn position. As an Italian female, I have learned that 84 bpm is fast enough for me to take a breath and walk away. The objective here is to connect to your body and make decisions about what you need before you get emotionally flooded. Once you're flooded, it's too late. You are looking for balance and the opportunity to respond and not react.

When you're operating from a relaxed and conscious state, you can make decisions, have conversations, and manage your day-to-day encounters without conflict or emotional inflammation. A relaxed conscious state also helps you to become more mindful of the present moment. Mindfulness is simply paying attention to the activity in front of you and fully participating in it. Driving is a good place to practice this awareness. How many times have you driven to and from work without thinking about having to make a left or a right turn? Driving can become an automatic process, but mindfulness while driving means to engage your senses, open the windows and feel the sensation of the wind on your face, listen to a song and sing out loud, and notice the sun or the moon or the stars. It's your ability to participate fully in the moment of whatever activity you're engaged in and not be entertaining your competing thoughts. Doing activities mindfully requires turning on your senses and turning off those competing thoughts. Empty your mind, access your senses—smell, touch, etc.—and notice everything.

Your mind will likely try to wander when you practice these exercises, so you must continue to redirect it. Use your breath and start focusing more intently on your inhale and exhale flow, counting the seconds spent on the inhale—*one, two, three, four*—as you fill your lungs to their maximum capacity and then slowly begin to exhale, counting in your mind again with *five, four, three, two, one.* And repeat. Write down your starting heart rate before engaging in this exercise, as well, and after two to five minutes of focused breathing, write down the results again. Continue working up to 20, 30, or 60 minutes of focused breathing as one of your meditative choices for grounding yourself.

Mindfulness practices help to reduce stress, so creating a discipline around them prevents you from flashbacking into dissociative states. They help you to stay ahead of your emotions by reducing feelings of sadness, anger, and depression. Mindfulness increases blood flow and helps strengthen your heart, keeping it healthy and promoting overall wellness. Mindfulness will take you to meditative states—passively or actively, too—and has been reported by people who lift weights, run, ride their motorcycle, or engage in other physical activities. One of my favorite ways to practice mindfulness is being tattooed. I've reached some of the deepest states of meditation during long sessions. Extensive tattoo work requires hours of sitting still while simultaneously having your flesh burned. On a pain scale, tattooing often registers high, and if your focus is on the physical pain, you will curse each moment in misery. If you instead choose to focus on your breath while playing relaxing music, you can direct your mind away from the physical pain and help your body release natural, pain-relieving endorphins. Music is another healing tool that has the power to access deeply rooted emotions. Challenge yourself to explore different activities that help you reach meditative states of emotional wellness.

Taking an integrative approach to your health and wellness requires understanding that healing is not a one-size-fits-all technique and oftentimes requires a multitude of different treatment options being used at the same time. Your only immediate task is a commitment to learning and providing yourself with tools to manage your mental health, rather than focusing on excuses to blame for your mental health. Being mentally well is saying: "I am aware and in control of myself despite whatever I've gone through or will go through because I know how to manage my emotional state." It's important to reiterate that, while treatment cures some symptoms, it doesn't prevent them from coming back, so accepting that you'll need to play an active role in staying well is very much part of that commitment you make to yourself. We have to work hard at holding onto our power and not allowing circumstances or the behaviors of others to throw us off; knowing that we'll be okay because we know what to do to manage ourselves is empowering. Most importantly, this process is about you learning that it's okay to feel and to have emotions; it's okay when they come to visit even though they sometimes suck, and it's okay to stay present even when it's not pleasant. It's also okay to keep growing and making adjustments to your standards and boundaries. You are allowed to continue to evolve.

Wellness and happiness are always accessible in the present moment if we choose to tune into these modes instead of battling the disappointment that comes with unmet expectations. That's the last part of maintaining a state of wellness: managing expectations and breaking up with "destination happiness." We can choose to access an element of happiness in every moment by looking for it instead of waiting for it to arrive. Happiness rarely arrives in quite the way we expect it to, so not managing your expectations can also contribute to your misery. This "destination happiness" I'm talking about surely started out with you having good intentions, but it also created a reality that is never quite good enough. We tell our kids that whenever they're having a hard time that it will get better, when in reality, they may always have a hard time with something—even when they're happy. We say things like, "Don't worry, it'll get better in middle school"—and then that experience is terrible, too, so we'll say "It'll get better in high school" only to have that be a complete nightmare, too, and so on. The mindset of "destination happiness" keeps you in the hot and heavy pursuit of happiness, never allowing you to slow down enough to say that there's happiness right here, right now, in the midst of the suck that life sometimes brings. There is happiness in the rising sun, the sweetness of ice cream, and the tenderness of a hug. There is happiness in all of the corners of life if we challenge ourselves to look for it. This new version of you is a person you love looking for happiness everywhere and feels gratitude upon finding it.

Gratitude practices are another way of intentionally setting your mind to focus on what's good by asking it to look for the good. I once worked with a coach who challenged me to experience 40 days of gratitude during a particularly difficult period of my life. He asked me to list three things I was grateful for every day and email them to him, counting the days in the subject line. Some days were harder than others, and I wrote things like "Nothing" as one of my items, and he would reply with "Look harder"—which then made me grateful for food that day or a warm bed to sleep in and clean water to drink. It's amazing how little you see when you feel crazy and are detached in a dissociative episode.

All of these daily practices can keep you from being hijacked by that emotional mind and lessen the amount of time you spend there when it does happen. The harder you work, the faster your recovery from those episodes will be. You'll recover faster because your brain is building a new neural pathway, and with repetition, that becomes a new rule for the operating system of your mind. That gratitude exercise I've just told you about was so profound for me that, to this day, the smell of lilacs stops me in my tracks wherever I am so I can take in their essence. This is called neuroplasticity, which is your brain's ability to change and adapt over the course of your life. It's the ability for you to explore and grow, and the more flexible you are with your thinking, the more receptive your brain will be to learning, no matter how old you are.

Be Happy in the Here and Now

> My dad just told me that the last time he cried tears of true happiness was when the Jets won the Super Bowl in 1969. I was born in 1988.

Briefly, we need to go back to destination happiness, which also has a way of creating an "It's too late" mentality. A "too late mentality" creates a belief system that causes people to not even try. They instead place restrictions on themselves due to their age or their relationship status or whatever else they see as a limitation to write off their ability to create whatever vision they have for themselves.

Please know that you can go back to school at age 40 or 60 to learn new skills or pursue a field more aligned with your passions. If there's anything worth pursuing in life, it's your passion, as passion also helps us tap into purpose, and a sense of purpose will help keep you alive during difficult moments. If you're struggling to find purpose, ask yourself, what would you be doing if you knew that you would not fail? This is an important question to ask often of yourself and of the different versions of you that evolve throughout your life. If you're feeling a sense of lack in your life or some void, look for the reasons why and ask yourself how, if at all, you are able to change things that are not working for you. When we accept that happiness is a state of being, we allow ourselves to pursue those things that will generate it within us.

This type of mindset will allow you to create the life you want to live and not just survive the one that you were given. "Why not you?" is another question to become comfortable asking yourself. "Why don't you deserve to be happy? To be successful? To be healthy? To be whatever sets your heart on fire?" When you answer those questions honestly, you will learn to let go of the expectations of how things were supposed to look based on what other people told you. You'll allow yourself to choose to create a reality that brings fulfillment and joy now instead of waiting until you graduate, get married, lose weight, buy a house, or whatever else they promised would make you happy.

Accessing joy in the present moment comes with allowing yourself to be yourself and letting go of the expectations placed on you. Stop living under heavy pressure and start living under realistic terms that can help you to stay connected to yourself. Be prepared to make permanent changes, too, because you may face resistance when you choose the healing path. You may find that the people in your life will not grow with you, and you may not be able to connect with them as you once did. This will bring you grief, and maintaining your new-found sense of self and emotional stability also means having the courage to say goodbye when you need to.

Allow others to be influenced by the way that you choose

to live your life. Achieving wellness is maintained through a great relationship with yourself, honoring and enforcing your boundaries, and holding people accountable to them. It's feeling empowered and having agency in your life, and it's knowing that you don't have to know everything because having people you can turn to for help is absolutely okay. Needing people in your life who are supportive and encouraging and asking for their help is all okay because you've learned to trust yourself, so now you can once again trust others. You know that it's okay to not be okay in the moment because you've also learned that all moments are temporary.

You're learning, slowly, to appreciate all of the moments for what they teach you, pay attention to the moments, be situationally aware, and choose what and with whom you engage. In the present moment, you see that you have options, and even if you don't always choose the right one, you know that you can choose again.

You will allow yourself to have a meaningful life by choosing to create and participate more fully in the one you were given. You are allowed as many defining moments as necessary to continue creating the best version of yourself. I hope this book has taught you about all of the different ways that mental health and wellness are impacted, and most importantly, that you may learn to respect, honor, and validate the traumatic experiences in your life so that you may offer the same to others. May you know that your story always mattered, what happened to you mattered, and how you feel about it will always matter, too. You are not defined by your past; it has no business in your present, and it doesn't define your future. Put aside your fears, identify those limiting beliefs, and continue to get the help you need to create your defining moments. May you create as many defining moments as necessary as you ascend the steps of self-awareness to mental stability and overall wellness.

Your mental wellness template begins with building a relationships worth having with yourself and then an honest inventory of your lifestyle especially in the areas that impact mental health the most: sleep, nutrition and movement. Building a healthy toolbox of skills involves having an open mind and trying new things. There are so many incredible treatment modalities to consider in achieving overall wellness. Other modalities to consider expanding upon your template include therapy, body work, breath work, yoga, self-help books, meditation, physical therapy, medical doctors, or reiki doctors, etc. You are to continue seeking opportunities to learn and grow into the best version of you; may that process be never ending and meaningful.

Meme Acknowledgements:

Listed in Order of Appearance

1. Megan@bodyposipanda_
2. Dr. Jenn@drjenpsychology
3. Janet Forklift @janetforlift
4. Aol.com@lucasbattle
5. Edward Burmilla @massforshutins
6. Molly@MollySneed
7. Bryan Russell Smith @bryan_r_smith
8. One Story Many Truths "unknown"
9. Alex @uhhdamn
10. 10a cartoon illustration
11. Emmers @hoegivesnofucks
12. Leigh Rubini Illustration
13. @TheArtidote Illustration
14. Axe Murderer @rmccarthyjames
15. Time to Write a New Story @mydefiningmoment
16. Jahnell Anya @JahnelleAnya
17. @itszils & @ merabichrayaar – user not found
18. @taishasuero
19. @asapbukake
20. Steven Bartett @stevenbartettsc
21. Laurent Perrier @itslaurenbwt
22. Kim Rose

23. Jessie@mommajessiec
24. Andrea Russett @andrearussett
25. Dad And Buried @dadandburied
26. Michael Adler, ESQ @madler9000
27. Hope Carpenter @hopepriestess
28. Barrett Luci @damnbluci
29. The Untastic Mr. Fritiz @unFitz
30. Eric Sprankle, PsyD @drsprankle
31. Kevin Flynn @whitepeoplehumor

Made in the USA
Monee, IL
06 September 2021

77469400R00111